The Disappearing

Policemen

Where they've gone, why, and how to get them back

J. G. Hicks

Copyright © 2025 J. G. Hicks

ISBN: 978-1-918038-53-8

All rights reserved, including the right to reproduce this book, or portions thereof in any form. No part of this text may be reproduced, transmitted, downloaded, decompiled, reverse engineered, or stored, in any form or introduced into any information storage and retrieval system, in any form or by any means, whether electronic or mechanical without the express written permission of the author.

Introduction

I decided I wanted to write a book about my experiences in the police. I don't know why it has to be now, I've been retired for over a decade. I served 1982 to 2012. Retired an Inspector. Surely all that stuff was by the by. Long gone.

But I've always written. I even wrote a 160,000 word novel once. I sent it to a few publishers and agents in a desultory sort of way, about fifteen years ago, not expecting them to be interested, and they didn't disappoint me. I've written quite a few short stories that I thought were good, but no one else did. I harboured frustrated ambitions to be the new Hemingway. In the meantime, I wrote articles on policing that were published in the now defunct "Police Review" in the nineties (no, I wasn't responsible for the publication's demise,) and have written articles on American policing for "Police Professional" magazine.

My idea was to write about all the things that had gone wrong with English policing since I retired. The police aren't as loved as they were, that's for sure. I have some pretty strong views about why that is, and the roots of the problem go way back into my time of service. I would say back to the early nineties. So, I decided to do some fieldwork. I spoke to my contemporaries, I spoke to people who joined in the seventies, some in the sixties. I even spoke to a retired Chief Constable and Assistant Chief Constable of my old Force. I sought out people that were still serving, and those that were instructing the new recruits. I had a lot of information. But I had no inspiration. No "in" to where I would begin the book.

I wrote an introduction that quoted satisfaction surveys and comments from venerated commentators on the state of English policing. I planned to draw on academic sources, to back up my ideas as to the routes to take for policing redemption. This would be a manual for redemptive change. But somehow this never seemed to work for me. Didn't tick the right boxes, to hold my interest. I interviewed most of my subjects in the autumn of 2022. I wrote a few lines, but it was meandering, not really enough to prompt me to get up at five, as I intended, write for a few hours until my wife rose, and we could begin the day.

I've been having dreams for quite a number of years, since I retired. They were all quite different, but all had the same theme. I was always still in the police, usually in roles that I had never served in. In the dreams I knew that I had thirty years in and could retire, but I was still there, sort of marooned. When I woke up from these dreams I was upset, disturbed that I seemed to be trying to tell myself something, but I couldn't make out what that something was.

Back in the spring of 1982 I was set to graduate from the University of Kent, with a mediocre degree in History and Political Science. In the summer of 1981 I'd met a girl at a factory where I was working during my summer vacation. One thing led to another and we wanted to get married. One day the following spring I'd seen an advertisement in the Guardian newspaper. Yes, I read the Guardian then, all students did. Become a police officer, it said, on the graduate entry scheme. You'll be an inspector in five years. In the end it took me sixteen, but that's a story for later. The Guardian advert spoke of a good salary and a free house, lots of other benefits. I had thought to train to be a history teacher. This police job meant that we could get married right away, and we'd have a house immediately. I applied.

I secured an interview at force level with the Chief Constable, and I was offered a job, then being put forward for the extended interview for entry onto the graduate scheme. To that end I spent three days at Sussex Police Headquarters at Lewes, just as Argentina prepared to invade the Falkland Islands. There were various ACPO ranks (Assistant Chief Constables and above) there for interviews, along with senior civil servants. I did badly, including telling a Deputy Chief Constable that his Force had handled picketing at a steel plant disastrously the previous year, during the national steel strike, not knowing that he was the architect of that plan. He was gracious enough to laugh. Needless to say, I failed to gain entry to the graduate scheme. I didn't have a clue. But I had a place to join as an ordinary constable, the lure of the free house was strong. So I did.

Was I cut out to be a police officer? I've thought about that a great many times in the last forty plus years. In the first few months of my service, at my first station after training school, I was asked by the Tutorial Sergeant, someone you visited once a month to test your law knowledge, if there was anything worrying me. I naively replied that I wondered how I would cope with the physical, violent aspects of the job as I hadn't had a fight since primary school. This Sergeant nodded sympathetically, then went immediately to the Chief Inspector, stating that PC Hicks had confessed to being a coward. I was called to see the said Chief Inspector, where I vehemently denied that was what I'd said. I learned a valuable lesson from that experience. Never confide anything to anyone that hasn't earned your trust through hard knocks.

That Sergeant was killed in a road accident about the time I was promoted to Inspector. I wish him no ill will. In a way I'm grateful to him as over the years he's made me think of the question of whether I was ever cut out to be a police officer? After all, I'd always planned to be a history teacher. Well, not always, but that's another and irrelevant story.

Police pay had been very uncompetitive in the sixties and seventies. Recruitment had been such a problem that, in 1977, the Callaghan Government had set up an enquiry into the mechanisms for setting police pay. The Enquiry, under Lord Justice Edmund Davies, recommended that the police should receive a whopping 45% pay rise. In May 1979, the incoming Conservative Government, implemented the recommendation in full. A police career immediately took on a lustre hitherto unknown.

That was the reason that I was drawn to the Job, that's how police officers refer to being a police officer, the Job. It was the money and the benefits. I knew many police officers during my service that wanted to a police officer since they were kids. Perhaps their father had been a copper, perhaps they liked the idea of exerting authority (contrary to received wisdom I never met many of those sort of people,) or perhaps they were motivated by the idea of public service. That wasn't me.

So, perhaps my motives for joining were not the most pure. But after teething troubles and negotiating a steep learning curve, I think I became a reasonable police officer and a competent supervisor. But my heart was always elsewhere. Don't misunderstand me. I became deeply committed to the job. I think I can say that I always did my best to serve the people of the communities I policed. There were coppers, especially in my early service, the residue of nineteen-seventies officers, who didn't leave when the pay was very poor, who were, what other cops called, "uniform carriers," those that wore the uniform, but didn't put themselves out to do anything else. Lazy bastards! I met one or two of those, they'd expend more effort to get out of doing any work than it would have taken to actually get on and do it. Again, I must emphasise that there weren't many of them.

So, I worked hard and did my best. Hand on heart. But if I could go back to 1982, and more specifically back to 1976, when I did rather well in my A levels, then stupidly decided not to take up a place studying history at the University of Warwick, I would have tried my all my might and main to have been a journalist and writer.

So, now that I've said all this, why should you read on? You should read on because I want to do something a bit different in this book. I want to tell you about some of the experiences I've had, the interesting people, both good and bad, that I've met over the years. I want to tell you my version of why the Job has taken a wrong turn, and what the current batch of officers have to do to turn it around.

Then I'm going to add some small pieces of fiction to the mix. These small pieces will try to illustrate the human side of being a copper. Yes, coppers are human and suffer the same doubts, fears, moments of resolution, and moments of irresolution, as anyone else. These pieces will not be completely invented. Each will have a nugget of truth from my own career in it.

There is no doubt at all that English policing has retreated somewhat from the noble objectives of preventing crime and keeping people safe. Policing today is a bureaucratic nightmare of box ticking, back covering and risk aversion, where senior officers, with little real-world experience, promote those that look like themselves, to perpetuate a regime that provides little reassurance and safety to the public they purportedly serve.

Please read on. I hope you enjoy the ride.

Doubt (Fiction)

My thoughts are often drawn back to the surviving archway of the old Theatre Royal in Nicholas Street, Weymouth. The archway existed in 1982, when I would pass by on my foot patrol. St Nicholas Street was dark and quiet, out of the way. I would go there when I needed escape from the noise, the catcalling, the danger of insult, the need to take action, when my feelings of doubt were strongest.

Red brick and topped with rolling stone cornices. It was a little forlorn archway to nowhere, shorn of its former glory as a gateway to colour, limelight and the sculpted word. Then, in my time, passing under its shadow would find you in a small car park, walled and forgotten. The colour and the light gone, absent from the memory of the people who leave their cars in this place, for their expeditions to Tesco, or for an idle coffee in some Esplanade cafe. Where once there was a stage, a proscenium arch, the banked rows of the auditorium, there are now Fords, Vauxhalls and Nissans, parked in neat rows.

As I stand here in the welcome cloak of darkness, I'm thinking about the audience, the actors, the performances that have illuminated the long forgotten stage, each one succeeding another in triumph. The ladies and gentlemen in their finery, parading, entering the brightness, caressing the red velvet of the spotless seats, the lights, the costumes and the skilfully annunciated words of the actors. It is said that the King had attended some performances here, the same King whose image is captured, carved from the chalk downs on the steep descent into town. The same King that had lost the American colonies. I thought of the now faded glory of the seafront Esplanade, of the great lords and ladies in its heyday, who would follow the King, standing faithfully back as he took the waters. All gone now. Remembered only as an idea. Their personalities, their characters, their being, submerged into a picture that only exists in my imagination.

And the theatre? There too, the dream ended, the windows boarded, the stage broken up, the actors gone and forgotten.

Then, later, the walls too were torn down. The only testament to the theatre ever having existed is this forlorn archway. I imagine one of those actors, a man I invented, the last to tread the boards here. I imagine him to be me, and my thinking comes around to how I'm only acting myself. Playing a part. I wonder how long this act can last, and what will happen to me when I take my last bow. I decide that this moment can't be long deferred.

Then my radio comes to life. An assistance shout, an officer in trouble in nearby St Thomas Street. Without thought I set off at a run.

Beginnings

"One of us only got married on Saturday." This from one of the other new recruits on that first Monday morning. There were three of us. I would learn that the other two were ex-Royal Navy. We were standing in a room at Force Headquarters, on that momentous first day. Ushered in and waiting for the rest. There would be ten of us in the end. Eight men and two women, a common proportion in those days.

I was the one who'd tied the knot two days before, so that my new wife and I could move straight into our police house. In those days no marriage, no house. In fact, no marriage, no living together. A great deal of your life was lived at the behest of Standing Orders, or the whims of senior officers. It seems strange today, but that's just how it was. There was no grievance procedure, no appeal procedures. You did as you were told. You liked it, or lumped it.

Now was the day when it all started. Thirty years if I made it. The Force Recruiting Sergeant cheerfully told us that most of us wouldn't. Spelling out in the first few days all the ways we could mess up. It turned out that it wasn't that bad. Eight out of ten of us made it through our probation. One man rented a video player, an outrageous luxury in those days, but inexplicably in another officer's name. He might have survived that, but, when his landlady found her soiled underwear under his bed, he was soon heading for the dole office. A female of our number couldn't resist the charms of a married member of her operational squad, finding herself pregnant, and an ex-police officer. All but one of the rest of us made it to thirty years. One of the ex-matelots, discussing my marital arrangement on the first day, transferred to a Welsh Force and retired on ill health grounds after a nasty car crash. Shame, he was a good guy, about six feet seven, a Navy field gun team member. The sort that you always hope would arrive first when you were experiencing a little physical bother.

That first week's schedule wasn't only pointing out the ways that, "Your services could be disposed of," as they phrased it. We were issued with our uniforms, and were told by the Recruiting

Inspector, in a plummy voice, that we looked like "ruptured ducks," as the Sergeant rolled his eyes behind him. The Inspector had been an officer in my Dad's draft to the Korean War, thirty years before. By all accounts he'd been kept well out of taking any responsibility for men in the line of fire, a fact that they were all, apparently, eternally grateful for. His Father was a member of the county set, and it seems that he'd progressed in the police, after leaving the army, more on account of that connection, than for any display of policing acumen.

The rest of the week was spent amending our Home Office Manual of Guidance. This thick binder would be our bible at Regional Training School, where we would spend the next ten weeks, mixing with recruits from the other forces in the region. Our method of amendment was quite quaint by modern standards. The amendments were on A4 sheets. We would cut out the relevant passage from the update with scissors, simply gumming it over the redundant section in the manual.

Then, the following Sunday, it was off to the Regional Training Centre. An old manor house in the North Dorset countryside. The five regional forces all used this facility. Within ten years it had been abandoned, sold off, as forces took responsibility for their own training. But, back in 1982, it was still going strong, staffed by trainers seconded from each of the five forces in the region. These instructors were the best turned out officers in the country. Boots bulled to shiny perfection, creases so sharp that you could cut a finger on them.

Drill and law. That's what we got every single day. Each morning, after breakfast, it was forming up in the quadrangle and marching smartly, well some were, some not so, down to the gravel frontage of the house. We were always in the same formation. The recruit in front of me had an alarming habit of swinging each arm in concert with the same side's leg. This is actually quite difficult to do, try it, but also very off putting when you're trying to keep in step yourself. Once on the gravelled area, before the grey portico of the house, we'd be marched around until it was time to be inspected by our course leader, a Wiltshire Chief Inspector by the name of Budd, a transferee from the Metropolitan Police. He was an intense, no nonsense type of character, who once told us gleefully, as he cradled his wooden truncheon, how during the Notting Hill riots of 1958, he and his colleagues had, "Put the rioters to the stick."

The ex-serviceman in our intake had no trouble with the drill, or the uniform care, but some of the rest of us struggled. As for me, I was okay at drill but, being an ex-student, whose idea of laundry was washing a shirt, then hang it in the wardrobe, hoping that the creases would drop out, mastering the crisp sharp creases necessary for the trousers, and the arms of the tunic, was problematic. But my biggest challenge was the boots. I just could not get a good bulled shine on them. Every morning Chief Inspector Budd would pass up and down our lines, held to stiff attention in the shadow of the towering manor house. As he came to me he would always chide me for some infraction. I remember him saying, "You"re in shit order, Mr Hicks," on many an occasion, as he grinned with his pinched bloodshot face. Only on one morning, in the ten weeks, did he pass by without criticising my turnout. On that morning he lingered for a long time in my face then, much to my surprise moved on. I'm sure I heard a mocking laugh as he sidled on up the line.

Self defence training was one lesson a week. The instructors admitted that they could teach us little, and when it came down to the crunch the outcome of any physical confrontation would be down to our own "grit and guts". Self defence, or Personal Safety Training, has always been a poor relation in the police training world. In general operational policing it was only one day a year, in which little of value could be taught. This was not due to the inadequacies or enthusiasm of the instructors, but simply the techniques taught required constant repetition to achieve efficiency. This was just not possible in the time available. Putting a "goose neck" hold on the wrist of a compliant colleague in a gym at headquarters, bore no resemblance to applying the same technique to an eighteen stone fighting mad drunk, on a wet side street, at two in the morning, in mid-January

The first aid training was also rudimentary, one short session a week. The problem was that the Home Office specified that a first aid exam had to be passed for a recruit to pass out and march triumphantly back to their force. This problem was solved in a very practical way. During our penultimate first aid training session, Fred Farrow, the flamboyant, ex-Royal Marine drill instructor, who doubled as first aid trainer, told us to take out our note books and take down twenty key words. The following lunchtime was the time for our first aid examination. We were all thrilled, and relieved, to discover that the twenty key words were the answers to the examination. Unbelievably, I still got a couple wrong!

Then there was the serious stuff, the law exams. Every week, on Monday morning there would be an examination to test each of us on the aspects of law we'd learned the previous week. The Theft Act 1968, The Public Order Act 1936, The Road Traffic Act 1972, and the Construction and Use Regulations made as statutory instruments under it. We were even taught when we had the power to inspect a pedlar's pack, under the provisions of the Pedlars Act 1871.

The questions in the examinations were all multiple choice, but they were tricky. One of the four answers would be obviously incorrect, the next would be probably incorrect, but the other two contained only a subtle difference between right and wrong. If a recruit failed three of these exams they would be nominated for failure, and faced the end of their fledgling police career, the final say being left to their force. It did happen sometimes, but, despite a couple of my fellow trainees being on two failures for the final exam, everyone on our course made it.

In contrast to my uniform travails, I passed all the exams without trouble and came top in the final exam. There was a prize for this, a dictionary donated by the Police Mutual Insurance Society. After the passing out parade, on the final day, I was presented with this volume before the assembled course, and our families, by my own Chief Constable, Brian Weight, who, by chance, happened to be the inspecting Chief Officer on the day. I've still got it, it's on my desk now, with an inscription dated, 8th October 1982.

The night before the passing out parade was our "dining in" night. A marvellous dinner, when our spouses, girlfriends or boyfriends (no, not boyfriends for the boys, this was 1982,) could come and be with us to celebrate our success. My wife came and spent the night in a local pub. No, I was not allowed to stay with her. I had to go back to my cold bed in the recruit accommodation.

I was brought back to earth the following Monday, as us Dorset recruits reassembled at Headquarters, for a two-week local procedure course. A visiting Sergeant lecturer quizzed us on our knowledge of Section 43(3) of the Bail Act. No one responded to his questioning, so he singled me out for special opprobrium for my ignorance, as he knew that I was the winner of the book prize. No one dare tell him that the Bail Act had not been one of the pieces of legislation that were on the syllabus at training school. You didn't argue with sergeants in those days.

Then, one Monday morning in late October 1982, I reported for duty at 0545hrs for my first early turn. The shift began at 0600hrs, but in those days you were expected to be there fifteen minutes early, and everyone duly complied. Later as a supervisor, I was always at shift thirty minutes early for handover, all unpaid of course. That morning I was due to be accompanied by my tutor constable, as I would be for my first four weeks. But on that first day my tutor had a day off, so I went out with someone else. My only recollection of my first shift was running after a horse that had become loose on a recreations ground.

Over the next four weeks I developed a great relationship with my tutor, Mick, with whom I carried out my first arrests. You'd think that the details would be forever engraved on my psyche, but I just remember that three lads had been ripping the wing mirrors from cars one dark night, being located in a small drinking hole nearby. The Sergeant told them that I was arresting them, and that was that. They all came without complaint or insult. Contrast that with my last arrest. Bournemouth in 2011, a man had been seen interfering with motor vehicles and I, the Duty Inspector, located him in the area, arresting him for vehicle interference. I placed him in the rear of my car, and as I waited for another officer to escort him into the nick, he began to tell me what he wanted to do to my wife and my children. Obscene would not encapsulate it. It wasn't pleasant, but sadly also not unusual.

Back in a dark autumn in 1982, it was around four in the morning. My tutor was driving us down a narrow country lane, near the small village of Portesham, just inland from the spectacular Fleet Lagoon. We had information that a man had been out during the hours of darkness, syphoning petrol from cars. It was quiet, deathly quiet. We were coasting along, the radio was silent, we were both tired and conversation had long since ceased. As I was about to drift into sleep the car veered to the left, and with a grinding jolt, began to climb the dry-stone wall bordering a field. My tutor had fallen momentarily asleep, but we were both very awake as we examined the damage to the Mark Two Ford Escort. The damage was extensive, but the car was still drivable.

In those days any driver involved in a POLAC, a police accident, was automatically suspended from driving. The Sergeant arrived with another PC, who wasn't the wisest of choices, as he too was suspended from driving after a previous POLAC. At that point in time I had taken a driving test with a Traffic Division Sergeant, but my authorisation to drive had not yet come through official channels. We had two cars, and only one authorised driver. The Sergeant made a command decision, instructing me to drive the car back to the station. These few short miles were the first of many hundreds of thousands that I must have driven in Job cars over the next thirty years.

Then, after four weeks with my tutor I was on my own. During those first few weeks walking the streets solo, the last thing you wanted to hear was your number being called on the radio. Today, new officers don't venture out on their own for a year. I'll admit that in the first few months I was clueless. Uniform shyness, the realisation that you are different from others, because of the blue uniform you wear, is very common. I certainly suffered from it. You're in the street, highly visible in the uniform and tall hat, as they used to call the helmet. Any member of the public calling you, relying on you, every bad guy that you confronted, had no idea if you have three months service, or ten years. They expected you to be an efficient police officer.

I think throwing new officers in at the deep end had many advantages, as long as the new officers had good sergeants and supportive colleagues to look out for him or her. Luckily, I did. On my squad, in my first few months, we had a great mix of probationers, PCs with between five and fifteen years service, the ones that knew the Job, and still had the enough enthusiasm to get things done, and old sweats who wouldn't go out of there way to catch a job, but who had the necessary nous and cunning to make sure that it went the right way if they did.

The default duty for the first two years was foot patrol. Hot in the summer, bloody cold in the winter. My Force had adopted a policy of allowing individual officers to make their own decision to go to shirt sleeve order, that is casting off your uniform tunic, in the summer, sleeves of the light blue uniform shirt to be rolled smartly above the elbows. One large force in the region had a policy that stated only the Chief Constable could authorise shirt sleeve order, after he came to duty in the morning. Early foot patrol in hot July must have been very uncomfortable.

Slowly I learned about arrests, traffic process, or reporting offending motorists for summons to court. Dealing with RTAs, Road Traffic Accidents, correctly logging and dealing with seized property. Plenty went on in my probationary period but it's not the purpose of this book to bore you with the day to day travails of an average "probbie," as probationers were affectionately, or not, on occasions, called.

But one incident that very nearly ended my police career and very nearly bore out what I'd heard on my first days in the job. Namely, how easy it was to find yourself in the shit, and swiftly out of the job. This incident, and its results, amply illustrate that there is no substitute in policing for experience, this incident being a particularly graphic example of that, as at the time I had very little!

It was a balmy summer's night in July 1983. I had been assigned to a rare mobile patrol on the North Panda area, that covered the sea front north of the town, along with the new housing estates, running along the main road out of the town towards Dorchester. At around three o'clock in the morning I drove into the large Lodmoor car park, used by many day trippers to the seaside. On that night it was empty, or not quite. As my headlamps swept from left to right I saw a car embedded in one of the wooden fences that separated the different areas of the car park.

On getting out of my car to investigate I was surprised to find an off-duty PC from another squad, who I will call Roy, standing next to the wrecked car. I asked him what had happened, to which he replied,

"I'm going to go for a TDA."

Accuse me of stupidity, by all means, naivety certainly, but I wasn't sure of his meaning at first. Of course, it's obvious now that he'd crashed the car and was going to claim that the car had been TDA'd, taken and driven away, by some other person. In my defence he didn't appear drunk, and my first inclination was to take him to the station to let more experienced heads sort this out.

On pushing through the back door of the station we immediately came across our avuncular Squad Inspector, a Welshman who wasn't averse to a few drinks himself. The offending PC wasted no time in relating his dodgy story to him, which resulted in me being told by the boss to record the crime. I think Roy realised what a tangled web he was falling into, protesting that he didn't want the crime recorded. The Inspector, of course, quite rightly, insisted, so I sat down with Roy in the parade room, writing the dodgy details of the fictitious crime in the blue crime book that we used in those days. Roy then went home to the flat he occupied behind the station.

If I'd followed procedure, I would have telephoned a recording machine at the Force Central Input Bureau, where, in the morning, a clerk would input the details onto the fledgling Force computer system. But instead of doing this I went to the Inspector, sitting at his desk in his office, his pipe wedged between his teeth, reading the local newspaper. I told him that I didn't believe that Roy's car had been stolen, setting in chain a course of events that would bring great sorrow to me, and, more fatally, to Roy. The Welshman's reaction are words that I still remember to this day.

"Oh, fucking hell!"

He ordered me to sit in the parade room and go nowhere, before dragging Roy back to the station, requiring him to give a sample on the Intoximeter machine, the machine that had largely replaced the need to take blood samples for evidential purposes from suspected drunken drivers. Roy was, of course, well over the limit.

That ill-fated night began a nightmare four months for me, when I strongly suspected that I would soon be out of a job, and consequently also out of place to live for me and my new wife.

As I've explained, the services of probationer constables could effectively be disposed of at any time in the two-year probationary period.

When my squad went home at 0600hrs that morning, I was ordered to sit in the office of the uniform aide, the lady that performed admin tasks for the uniformed officers of the station. I forlornly perched on a chair in that room, no one seemed to take much care or notice of me. Later in the morning the kind-hearted uniform aide took pity on me, making me a cup of tea and buying me a Kit Kat. Her named was Di, and for those small acts of mercy, I will always be grateful to her. But to everyone else, I was obviously damaged goods.

At around two o'clock in the afternoon a Detective Chief Superintendent from Headquarters, along with a Detective Inspector, interviewed me under caution. By this point I hadn't had any sleep for over twenty-four hours. I hardly knew what day it was. Today, it would be unlawful to treat even a criminal in such a manner.

After this ordeal I was allowed to go home to confess my ignominy to my wife. I went to bed at around four pm. An hour or so later I was woken up by a phone call, from my Sub-Divisional Commander, the Superintendent in charge of my station. He informed me that the Deputy Chief Constable, the officer in charge of Force discipline, had decided not to suspend me. I think it was at this point I realised the seriousness of my position.

During the four-month period in limbo, the period between the incident and the time I learned that my job was no longer in jeopardy, I many times considered resigning and doing something else. This was a big decision to make, not least because, as I've said, such a move would render my wife and I homeless. In October I gave evidence against Roy in magistrates court. He was convicted of wasting police time and driving with excess alcohol, and in a later discipline hearing, required to resign. I had been served with discipline notices, alleging that I had fraudulently completed a crime book, additionally I was in neglect of duty as I hadn't made an entry in my pocketbook in relation to the incident. My reasoning, as far as that goes, was that it was better to write nothing than to write a compendium of stupidity.

Later, I was interviewed by a Detective Chief Superintendent in relation to the alleged discipline offences. I'll change his name to Smith, as I believe he lives still. He was humourless and overbearing, everything a good boss is not. When the interview was over, one rainy afternoon, my Inspector, the same Welshman that had dragged Roy back to the station to end his career, came back to the station to pick me up and drive around on patrol for a few minutes. It was an act of support, I was in no doubt of that. As we drove out of the police station yard he turned to me and said.

"Well John, how was that cunt Smith?" It was his way of telling me he was on my side. I've never forgotten that.

In late autumn I was called to Divisional Headquarters to appear in front of a Chief Superintendent and learn my fate. I was ushered into his office and told to sit down. He was very relaxed.

"I understand that I've got to tell you off," he said, smiling "Okay, you're told off." He then told me what I should have done on that night four months before. He told me that I should have just taken Roy home, telling him to reappear late next morning, nice and sober. From the vantage point of the twenty-first century this may well appear shocking, police covering for police, closing ranks. Yes, I agree. But this was forty years ago. I know of an Inspector, not the Welsh one, who took at least two police drink driver's home in similar situations. In these cases, no member of the public had been harmed or involved. If they had been then the offender would have been on his own. Whatever your current moral view, that's just the way things were.

It is difficult to justify, and I've often wondered what I would have done if I'd come across a similar situation again. I would feel little sympathy for any police officer suffering the consequences of drink driving. It would be impossible to make a case for covering up for an officer involved in thieving. What's the difference? The question is made more opaque in my mind by the knowledge that it would have been difficult for me to remain working at that station, maybe the Force, if I had breathalysed Roy that night. The point was that by his own actions he ultimately sealed his fate.

After that my probation was fairly free of controversy. In April 1984 I went back to the District Training Centre for my two week Continuation Course. This Course was mainly concerned with police action in the event of nuclear attack. A not too unlikely fear at that time during the Cold War. The message seemed to be that the authorities knew that, in the event of the balloon going up, we'd all probably desert our posts, going home to do what we could for our families. But it was necessary to remind us that police stations would be the storage centres for food and medical supplies. We'd be more use to our loved ones if we stayed at our posts, to do our duty. Yes, of course we'd do that. Eyes to heaven.

One positive aspect of this course was that we'd parade once each week with the initial recruits. As we marched out past them the Drill Sergeant would shout,

"Look at them, they've been doing the Job for two years, they're real police officers." Our chests would swell with pride as we wheeled around and processed before the green recruits.

The month before I trailed reluctantly back to the Training Centre the National Union of Mineworkers had called a national coal strike. The strike would last a year, the reverberation of it would shape the last couple of months of my probationary period, and on until the end of winter of the following year. I'll come back to this momentous year for British policing later in the story.

Why Do Patrol?

One summer's night in 1986, my probation safely behind me, I was on night duty, having been detailed to patrol the West panda area, as it was called. It was an area extending from the town centre, through the Weymouth suburb of Wyke Regis, to the Isle of Portland causeway. The area was made up of mostly Edwardian housing that, at the time, was experiencing a spate of night-time burglaries. I had abandoned my panda car in a side road and, just as wiser old heads had taught me, had been creeping around on foot, no cap, my blue uniform jacket and trousers blending nicely into the puddles of shadows cast by the street-lamps. I'd spent twenty minutes crouched in the garden gateway of a property perched on a steep hill. But nothing was moving.

The current theory was that the burglars were using the disused railway line, mostly passing through the area in a culvert, to move around undetected. With this in mind, at around two-thirty am, I crept, as stealthily as I could, to the seaside, where the culvert issued out into a bridge over Portland Harbour. I hunkered down under a clump of bushes. After about ten minutes I'd decided to move again, but then, out of the darkness, two figures in dark clothing came towards my hiding place. They were talking quite openly to one another, clearly oblivious to my presence. Then, as they drew nearer, betraying both my optimistic nature and my naivety, I emerged from my hiding place shouting, "Police, stand still!" with as much authority as I could muster, snapping on my torch into their startled faces. They turned and ran, becoming lost in the orange lights of Portland Naval Base in the distance. A few seconds later I found one of them hidden in some outcrops of gorse. He offered no resistance at all, and I duly arrested him, rather tenuously, on suspicion of burglary.

Back at the station it soon became evident that my prisoner was dressed in grey prison uniform. He wasn't a burglar (on this occasion) but was, in fact, a convict who'd escaped from the prison, HMP Verne, on Portland. His mate was arrested the next day, in nearby Dorchester.

What is my point in relating this unremarkable episode to you? Well, I caught that escaped prisoner because I was there. Of course. Yes, you may say. So what? My point is that today, I, or a much younger version of me, would not be there. The police of the second decade of twenty-first century do not patrol. A police spokesman will always reassure the community that, "Patrols have been stepped up," in the face of some high-profile crime. What this really means is that a few officers will make themselves highly visible in an area for a couple of days, then disappear again, back to doing whatever they spend their time doing nowadays. As journalist and social commentator, Peter Hitchens comments in his 2003 book, "A Brief History of Crime," it is like, "The enforcement of the law has become a concession granted by the authorities from time to time, not a right enjoyed equally by all."

Let's suppose that a crime has been committed, for example a violent street robbery, during which an elderly lady has been pushed over, her handbag being ripped from her grasp. These "stepped up patrols" can't undo the harm that the crime has caused. The broken hip, the skinned arms and legs, the emotional toll, the feeling that she will never be safe in public again. But the "stepped up patrol" idea has within it a nugget of truth. When a uniformed police officer is present in a location, criminals are deterred from committing crime, due to risk of being apprehended and suffering punishment. That's so obvious that it doesn't need saying. If only that was true.

Although I performed most of my service in operational policing, I did spend three short periods at Force Headquarters, working on the theoretical side of the Job. I became very familiar with the works of great criminologists, like the American Herman Goldstein and our very own Professor Robert Reiner, from the London School of Economics.

In 1979 Criminologists, Lawrence E. Cohen and Marcus Felson, published an article in the American Sociological Review entitled, "Social Change and Crime Rate Trends: A Routine Activity Approach." The article examines the rise in crime in American cities in the post war years. Like most academic approaches to real world problems "Routine Activity Theory" is simplicity rendered into complexity. Amid the abstruse discussion of "Human Ecological Theory," and, "spatial temporal organisation of social activities," they posit a simple truth. "Most criminal acts require convergence in space and time of *likely offenders, suitable targets,* and the *absence of capable guardians."* In other words, if a crook sees a likely victim and there's a police officer (capable guardian) at the scene, or nearby, they will be less likely to commit the offence. Obvious or what? But clearly not to police managers since the early 1990s.

The question is, if beefed up patrols in an area after a high-profile crime prevents further such crime, why not do it all the time, like police in England did until the waning of the twentieth century? That is a simple question, with a complicated answer. But first Let's look back at why the early proponents of policing thought that routine preventative patrol was a good idea.

At 6 pm on Tuesday, the 29th of September 1829, the first constables of the Metropolitan Police set out on patrol. The force had been brought into being by the Home Secretary, Sir Robert Peel in the Metropolitan Police Act of 1829. The measure was intended to bring together the fragmented old system of local watches and constables. There was also a perception that crime was on the increase, and a new modern approach was required to address it.

Arguably the most famous living police chief in the world is William Bratton, the man who is credited with engineering the great crime decline in New York, as Commissioner of the New York Police Department between 1994 and 1996. He went on to become Chief of the Los Angeles Police Department, between 2002 and 2012, before returning for a second stint at the NYPD from 2014 and 2016. He was even approached by David Cameron in 2011, with a view to becoming Metropolitan Police Commissioner, but fell foul of the rule that stated that the holder of that post must be a British subject. More's the pity, I say.

It may seem strange that I've introduced Bill Bratton when initially talking about Sir Robert Peel and the founding of the Metropolitan Police one hundred and ninety-four years ago. Let me explain. I have read many articles penned by Bratton, seen him speak in numerous forums about his founding policing principles. In his 2021 memoir, "The Profession," he tells of a meeting that he, and other new sergeants had with the then Metropolitan Police Commissioner, Sir Robert Mark, in 1975 when Sir Robert visited Bratton's first police department in Boston. Mark spoke to the young Bratton about Sir Robert Peel and "Peel's Principles." Bratton was unaware of these principles up to that point, but since then he has made them the bedrock upon which he has based all his police commands.

Speaking at the memorial lecture to the eminent criminologist George Kelling in 2020, Bratton opined on his career long adherence to these principles. "I would argue the Father of Democratic Policing (Peel) put forth nine principles of policing that are my Bible, the foundation of everything that I, and I believe George (Kelling), built our careers upon..........If you think of those nine principles ...... written in 1829, they're as relevant, and maybe even more relevant, in 2020 than they were back then."

So, what are these principles, these Bible tenets of the most admired police officer of the last thirty years. Well, in all likelihood they weren't Peel's principles at all, but those of Charles Rowan and Richard Mayne, the first joint Commissioners of the Metropolitan Police. Rowan was a military man, wounded at Waterloo, whilst Mayne was an eminent barrister. Both were born in Ireland, Mayne became the first solo Commissioner in 1856, serving until his death in 1868. It was probably he who drew up the policing principles so admired by Bill Bratton.

There are nine of these principles. The very first is absolutely crucial to the role of any police organization, and, in my humble opinion, the key to why the modern police force has so lost its way.

"The basic mission for which the police exist is to prevent crime and disorder."

Nowhere in these principles is there any mention of detecting crime or locking up offenders. No mention of detection rates or persons brought to justice.

In July of 2023 the public learned the shocking news that police in England and Wales detected only 27% of burglaries in 2022/23. In the Metropolitan Police area this figure was a paltry 18%, only propped up in the league of shame by South Yorkshire (16%) and Hampshire (17%). A spokesperson for the Met took some solace in the fact that officers now attend 9 out of 10 burglaries. A pertinent question, in light of the detection figures would be, to what end?

I confess, I have little time for politicians whatever colour rosette they wear, but the hackneyed cliches rolled out by the overpaid and underworked of Westminster in response to these figures, made even jaundiced old me roll my eyes. "We will boost detection rates if we get into power." "We will give a guarantee that all burglaries will be attended by police." Then there's the old chestnut of community policing that is always sandwiched into any discussion of these matters, a concept that all parties endorse, but none appear to understand.

The facts are that the public would much rather that their house wasn't burgled, or their shop window broken, or be assaulted when they ask rowdy drunks to be quiet at three o' clock in the morning. They want the police to do exactly what Richard Mayne described in his first principle. They want the police to prevent crime and disorder.

So how can this be done. In 1829 Peel's first 1,000 Metropolitan Police officers were expected to know their beat intimately, and be able to cover that whole beat area in ten to fifteen minutes, at a slow pace of three miles an hour. In his excellent book, "The Great British Bobby," police scholar Clive Emsley gives a pertinent example of how a patrolling PC with knowledge of his beat can prevent crime. PC Hennessy was patrolling his beat in the Rathbone Place area of Central London on the 5th July 1861. Hennessy saw Robert Shepherd, a known criminal known as "Shepherd Hoppy," due to his lame right foot, loitering in a passage between streets at 10-20pm. PC Hennessy again encountered Shepherd ten minutes later and, surmising that he may loitering for a criminal purpose, told him to be on his way. Shepherd objected saying that it was not a late hour to which Hennessy replied, "Whether it is a late hour or not I shall not have you about here, I shall see you away." Hennessy followed the limping felon until he left the area. Crime prevented.

Recorded crime in Victorian London did take a dramatic dip, after the first police officers took to the streets in 1829, and through the rest of the nineteenth century. Of course, crime statistics in those times were far from reliable, and social attitudes may well have as much or more of an impact on crime, particularly violent crime, than the new police. But there is evidence that highly visible, motivated uniformed police officers do deter crime in an area, and there is also a great deal of evidence that such patrols have a positive effect to reduce the fear of crime.

In 1965, Home Office official J. A. Bright carried out an experiment in four British cities in which foot patrols in a particular area were varied between 0 and 4 officers. When there were officers on foot patrol the crime rate declined. This was a very limited study. To drill down more deeply we must go to the United States.

Going back to 1954, the New York Police Department conducted an experiment called Operation 25, after the Manhattan 25th precinct covering most of East Harlem, where it was carried out. The Operation lasted four months and police foot patrols in that area were doubled. The results were dramatic. Street robberies declined from sixty-nine in the same period in 1953 to seven. Theft of cars from seventy-eight to twenty-four. In the early seventies The Police Foundation evaluated the Newark Foot Patrol Experiment in New Jersey. As George L. Kelling and Catherine M. Coles note in their book "Fixing Broken Windows," in the areas covered by the experiment,

"Fear declined and citizen appreciation for the police soared.......Residents of foot patrolled areas felt more secure than did those in other areas."

Another added benefit that was noted was,

"Foot officers, in turn, were more favourably disposed towards citizens in their neighbourhoods and experienced higher morale than did their colleagues who patrolled in cars."

In 2005, economists Klick and Taborrok, found that an increased police presence in the national Mall in Washington DC led to a significant decrease in crime. Klick and criminologist John MacDonald studied increases in private police patrols around the University of Pennsylvania. They found that crime not only dropped significantly in that area, but also in city blocks nearby.

In 2009 researchers from the Department of Criminal Justice at Temple University, Philadelphia, carried out an experiment in the Philadelphia Police Department. A focus on 60 crime hotspots revealed that intensive foot patrol radically cut violent crime in those areas targeted. Studies were carried out in a number of other US cities, Boston, San Diego, Oakland amongst many others. All reported that either crime had been reduced, and that citizen fear of crime had diminished.

My first posting after training school in October 1982 was to foot patrol in Weymouth town centre. We would parade an Inspector, 3 Sergeants and around ten PCs on a good day, either 0600hrs earlies, 1400hrs lates and 2200hrs nights. One sergeant would be the station sergeant, answering citizens queries in the enquiry office, and looking after any prisoners that were brought in under arrest. Looking after prisoners would be a part time job until 1986, when the Police and Criminal Evidence Act 1984, required that the sergeant would act as a custody officer, and his, or her's, full time job would be the processing and welfare of these prisoners.

If you were allocated a foot beat you would walk to town, a good twenty-five minute walk from the station, then walk back again for your forty-five minute meal break. Then back to the town again, then back to book off duty. Going off your beat was strictly forbidden, unless given leave to do so by the Sergeant, and speaking to the officer on the adjacent beat, when your paths crossed, was not allowed. Sometimes, on the coldest nights, the Sergeant would pick you up in his car to give you a "warm up." Then back out on patrol. I had one woman Sergeant, a lovely lady, but who had a very heavy nicotine habit. When she picked up you would always leave her car reeking of tobacco.

The system worked well. You got to know people and places on your beat, and the wrong 'uns, who you kept an eye on. As a probationer constable, that is one in the first two years of your service, when you could be fired without reason, you were encouraged to submit a piece of process at every shift. That is some infraction for which the offender would be summonsed to court, known as "process." A fecund area for process was cycling. Riding on the pavement, riding with no lights. In those days even these offences were prosecuted, and, if a guilty plea was not entered, then an appearance in court was standard.

One damp, dark evening I was traversing St Thomas Street at the regulation pace, when a man cycled towards me against the one-way street order, not displaying a single light. I stopped him, pointed out the offences he was committing, telling him that he would be reported for summons. A few weeks later I found myself in Weymouth Magistrates Court giving evidence against him, as he had denied it all. In the witness box I read from the notes in my pocket-book, drawing a smile from the magistrates, when I informed them that when I'd cautioned the man he'd replied, "Hokey Cokey."

The man then took to the witness box in his own defence, denying he'd been riding the cycle against the traffic, baldly stating that he was displaying lights to the front and rear, in full compliance with the law. As was common in those days the magistrates believed me, the police officer, finding the miscreant guilty, fining him a small sum. He approached me in the foyer after the proceedings and, shaking my hand, admitted lying. He added, "You've got to try it on, haven't you?" He laughed, thought for a moment, then quipped, "I did say Hokey Cokey didn't I? You got that right as well."

I tell this trivial story because it gives the flavour of the nature of preventive policing, until the late nineties when it all went wrong. Okay, I prevented that man from riding his bike home on a rainy night. When he went around the corner he would have got back on, riding home, still, lightless. I know that. So what?

On the gloomy cold Sheffield night of January 2nd 1981 Sergeant Bob Ring and PC Robert Hydes of South Yorkshire Police, were on patrol in the red light area of Broomhill. They checked a Rover V8 car parked in Melbourne Avenue. In the driver's seat was a bearded man, in the passenger seat was a 24 year old prostitute named Olivia Reivers, who Sergeant Ring knew from previous dealings. One of the officers used his radio to contact the Force Police National Computer Bureau. His check revealed that the registration plates on the car related to a Skoda, not a Rover. The officers examined the plates, finding that they had been attached over the real registration plates using black tape. The bearded man was arrested on suspicion of theft of the plates. Such a check was common in those days, producing many arrests.

The bearded man asked to be allowed to go into the bushes to relieve himself, which I'm rather surprised Sergeant Ring allowed without supervision. On arrival at the police station with their prisoner, the officers became suspicious of the man, as he matched the physical description of the most wanted man in all Great Britain, the killer dubbed the Yorkshire Ripper, who had brutally murdered and defiled women across Northern England since 1975. The next day Sergeant Ring returned to the area where the man had urinated, discovering a discarded knife, rope and hammer. By the 4th January, that man, Peter Sutcliffe, had confessed to the murder of thirteen women. So ended the largest manhunt in the history of these islands.

So, who had finally been responsible for the apprehension of the infamous Ripper. The teams of experienced detectives, who had been working doggedly, amongst the ever growing mountains of statements and intelligence reports, for over five years? The legions of forensic officers, who painstakingly combed the scene of each dreadful killing, or the highly skilled Home Office pathologists, who attended to do their grisly work on the bodies of each unfortunate woman? No, it was two uniform officers, who were actively patrolling their area, looking for the out of the ordinary, the mundane irregularities in everyday life. Those that required investigation. It's said that a good police officer is nosey. These two officer's nosiness paid dividends. They certainly prevented the murder of the young woman, Olivia Reivers, and probably others in the future.

Today, they wouldn't be there. Those mundane irregularities would go un-investigated. A modern-day Sutcliffe would probably be able to pursue his dreadful work without interference from nosy patrol police officers, because officers no longer patrol as they used to.

In the case of my jovial, but unlit cyclist, what if, instead of being a devil may care comedian, he'd been furtive and evasive, I would have probed further. Perhaps, if I could elicit the required reasonable suspicion, I would even search him. He may have been in possession of an offensive weapon, on his way to assault a rival, or carrying stolen goods, en route to a fence, a person that receives stolen articles.

But, highly visible policing has another benefit, being summed up in the second leg of the first of Peel's principles.

*"The basic mission for which the police exist is to prevent crime **and disorder**."*

The effects of disorder have, perhaps, a much more deleterious effect on the quality of life in an area than crime. An area plagued by disorder has little social cohesion. The writ of law does not seem to extend to it. People indulge in public drinking to excess. They swear at and harass pedestrians. Youths gather on street corners, mocking and abusing law abiding people, as they hurry by on the way to work, or on their way to visit family members. Drug abusers live in tent encampments on the streets, public urination and defecation is common. People begin to keep children in, not allowing them to play together on the streets and parks, as they have a right to do, as such spaces have been taken over by drug dealers, street drinkers and the homeless. The communal areas of flats and housing developments are avoided by the community, as they have become menacing and unpleasant to inhabit. The fly tipping of rubbish and discarded drug paraphernalia, become the norm in stairs wells and landings. The world becomes an environment that must be endured, rather than one to be enjoyed.

Anthropologist Michael Banton in his 1964 work "The Policeman in the Community" observed that,

"The policeman on patrol is primarily a 'peace officer' rather than a 'law officer.' Relatively little of his time is spent enforcing the law in the sense of arresting offenders; far more is spent 'keeping the peace' by supervising the beat and responding to requests for assistance."

Any police officer, that has spent any time at all on the streets, knows that the majority of calls from the public have little, or nothing, to do with serious crime, or indeed any crime at all. Many are cries for help from the community to help address minor community disorder. The kids drinking alcohol on the street corner, being abusive to passers-by. The fly tipping of rubbish at a beauty spot. The neighbour who hosts parties well into the night on work days. Problems that blight the lives of residents of the neighbourhood, but are unlikely to stimulate the concerns of politicians, too busy issuing grandiose statements about burglary detection rates, or burnishing their law and order credentials.

My daughter is a singer. She sings in pubs and clubs, at weddings and other functions, mostly in the large South Coast town where she lives. One Saturday afternoon she was singing in a very large town centre pub, in one of the busiest shopping streets of the town. My wife and I attended to watch her. I started to chat to one of the security staff, I asked him if he ever saw patrolling uniform police, as he stood on the door during the day. His answer startled me, as I knew that in the eighties, this particular town centre, would regularly deploy over a dozen foot patrols during the day. He told me that, although he stands outside for most of his work time, he never sees a patrolling officer walk by on foot patrol. He also told me that the pub had given up calling police when a patron attempts to use a stolen bank card, as the control room staff invariably state that officers are too busy to attend. On a roll by this time, he told me that the week before an assault had occurred on the opposite side of the street from the pub. He and a colleague had detained the offender, only to be told by the police control room that they had no one to send. Large stores and small ones in the town centre, he complained, had given up calling the police to shoplifters, as such a call elicits no police response.

I was in my own town centre with my wife a few months ago when I heard a commotion break out nearby, in a pedestrianised part of the High Street. I listened with interest as, after all, I'm a nosy ex-police officer. It seemed that a man, accompanied by his wife and child, had discarded a cigarette butt onto the ground, rather than in a bin. A man, a civil enforcement officer, the employee of a private company, contracted by the council to enforce by-laws against littering, in exchange for a fee for each fine levied, was demanding the man's details.

Advance disclosure. I hate littering, and I hate smoking too. But while I watched this private contractor attempting to obtain the personal details of the offending smoker, two things occurred to me. Firstly, why should a private citizen have to disclose their personal details to a private contractor who, after all, has no statutory power to demand them, and therefore no lawful mandate to require anything of that private citizen.

The second revelation occurred in the ten minutes or so that I was watching them. In that time three cyclist barrelled by me on the crowded pedestrianised High Street, scattering pedestrians to left and right. No effort was made by the council enforcement officer to stop these cyclists, indeed he would have no power to do so. These cyclists could run down a small child, or an elderly person, causing significant injury, or even death. Well, never mind, at least the smoker would have to pay a fine that would make him regret his casually discarded dog end.

If you're a discerning reader you may be saying as you read this. So, you're in favour of "Zero Tolerance Policing" are you? Police arresting or taking to court anyone for any minor infraction. That seems draconian, even totalitarian. No, I'm not advocating that. Let me explain.

When Bill Bratton headed the NYPD in the early nineties, and turned the city of New York from a crime hot spot to a mecca for tourists and a pleasant place to live for residents, there was some confusion when some commentators muddled up "Zero Tolerance Policing" with "Broken Windows Policing."

"Broken Windows" is a theory that burst upon the world in an article by criminologists George L. Kelling and James Q. Wilson in the Atlantic Monthly in March 1982. A simple example of this approach is the situation where a building has one window broken. If nobody fixes it this leads over time to the impression that no one cares about the building, and such damage will be tolerated. Then, those with a destructive bent, will break more windows, then more, until the area around the building sinks into crime and disorder. But if the window is promptly fixed, an aura of order and stability is projected. In an area where people appear to care about the state of their neighbourhood, there is stability and safety.

New York's 1990s renaissance was achieved by a combination of Broken Windows, and Zero Tolerance. Graffitied subway trains were repainted within 24 hours, public parks were cleaned up, and dilapidated neighbourhoods invested in, re-energised. But on the other hand, beggars were cleared from the streets, fare dodgers on the subway were arrested, a trivial offence maybe, but many of those arrested were found to be wanted on warrant for serious offences, like robbery or firearms infringements. The situation was so bad at that time in the city that extreme measures were justified. This was a city that, in 1990, was experiencing over two thousand murders a year. By the end of that decade that number had dropped below seven hundred. By 2018 that figure was 289, the lowest figure since 1951.

In a conversation with the Reason Podcat, on 15th March 2023, Bill Bratton spoke about Broken Windows Policing. He corrected his liberal host, who had conflated Zero Tolerance Policing with Broken Windows Policing, clearly being under the impression that Broken Windows came with an inbuilt draconian arrest regime. Bratton corrected him,

"If you see crime you take action, that action doesn't have to be in an arrest, that action can be a summons, can be a citation, can be an admonishment."

The point is that some action must be taken, in most cases short of arrest. Perhaps by telling reckless cycle riders in pedestrian zones to get off and push it, or issuing them with a fixed penalty ticket. Low level disorder cannot be allowed to flourish unaddressed, or it will metastasise into something of a much more serious nature.

But to have the ability to take action there has to be the third element of the Routine Activity Theory that I spoke about earlier. *The capable guardian.* The police officer on foot patrol or perhaps motor patrol, not simply taking them to the next crime scene, but being vigilant and aware of their beat, and willing to take action.

I hope that I've convinced you of the absolutely fundamental value of the patrolling police officer, in keeping everyone safe, and the streets crime and disorder free, a pleasant place to be. I consider this fact obvious, and I believe so should so many senior officers who could make it happen. So why are they not doing so? More on that later.

Progress (Fiction)

It was 1976. I remember it because it was that summer. You know, the one that was as hot as hell, that went on forever, well, not forever. Nothing lasts forever. I was a probationer, a new guy. Someone who just kept quiet and did what his tutor told him. If he had any sense, and I did, I prided myself on it. Did me well over the years. I just kept quiet and got on in the job. Knew all the right answers to all the right questions. Finished high up, with a good pension. I was only on the streets for a few years, that's the way to do it. Less chance of having to do something difficult, something unpredictable. Getting yourself in a position that will fuck up your chances to get on in life.

On that particular shift, I was out with my tutor on nights, in a van, just the two of us. In those days you spent four weeks with your tutor, then you were on your own. Sammy Davis, that was my tutor's name. Huge guy with big apelike arms and a head as big as a basketball, well nearly. I suppose he should have been nicknamed Junior, but no one had the nerve. Sammy was not the sort of guy that you messed with. If he was your tutor and he told you to jump, you only asked how high. Even the Sergeant was wary of him. Just before I came on the shift a new Inspector, who hadn't heard about the nature of Sammy, had told him to arrest someone at a big fight. Sammy's verdict was that the fight was over, no one was too hurt, so everyone should just go on their way. He told the Inspector to arrest the bloke himself if he felt like it, as he wasn't going to. The Inspector made a big fuss, but nothing happened to Sammy. That was how it was in those days. When I got on, I made sure that people like Sammy knew their place. But that's another story.

So, we were outside a nightclub at about one or so. A big guy, about six two, had been ejected for harassing women inside, and he was erring on the size of being gobby. You know lippy. He was failing the attitude test, as Sammy used to describe it. Good attitude, go on your way. Bad attitude, in the van you go. This Mr Gobby wasn't looking to get punchy though. Even I, new to the game as I was, could see that. He had sort of a clever, do you think I'm amusing, look on his face.

"You bouncers would be okay if you weren't eunuchs," he told them. His voice seemed too high for his body somehow, like he was pretending to be someone he wasn't. Sammy told him in no uncertain terms to fuck off, or he'd find himself in trouble. He didn't seem to want to take that advice, and just stood his ground, making what he thought were smart remarks like,

"Is your head that shape under that hat?" Even I'd heard that too many times already for it to be funny.

Sammy clearly wasn't impressed by his wit either. Picking the geezer up by the shirt collar, he threw him down the road like a bag of old rubbish. He ended up in an untidy heap in the gutter, much to the bouncer's loudly expressed amusement.

But this bloke seemed to be a glutton for punishment. Within a few seconds he'd dragged himself off the ground, hurrying back, right in Sammy's face.

"Look what you've done to my shirt." His lovely mint green Ben Sherman had a long rip down the arm. "You're going to have to pay for this, you fucking cunt."

Well, this was way beyond Sammy's tolerance threshold. He threw me the van keys, shouting at me to open the back doors. Mr Gobby was soon lying on the dirty rubber matting of the van floor, having been propelled inside by Sammy, by means of his ruined shirt collar and trouser waist.

I had apparently arrested him for being drunk and disorderly, so I joined him in the van, Sammy locking the door behind me. By this time my prisoner had dragged himself off the floor, slumping himself down opposite me on the bench seat running along the side of the van. His posh shirt was now totally wrecked, hanging limply off his grazed and bleeding shoulder. He was a very sorry looking gentleman. But, just for now, a quiet one.

We were about halfway back to the nick when Mr Gobby came out of his trance, and really began to give Sammy what for. It started with what a cunt Sammy was, but then graduated to what a sorry bitch his wife must be to marry him. But it was, "Tell her to come around to me one night and I'll show her what a real man can do," that seemed to be the straw that broke the camel's back.

I became aware that the van had stopped, and that Sammy was very slowly, very deliberately, walking around to the back, unlocking and opening both doors to their full extent. He never said a word. Mr Gobby was now silent. He was looking at Sammy with a sort of apologetic smile, an almost "you're not taking me too seriously are you mate?" look. Sammy turned his head and looked around, for a moment I considered the idea that he was going to let the guy go. He was just proving too much hassle. How little I knew in those days?

Then, it happened so quickly, it was almost as if he was outside and inside the van at the same time, Sammy launched himself in, punching Mr Gobby in the face so hard that I was splashed with his sweat as he collapsed down, onto the filthy floor of the van. The sound of the punch, a thud, like a wooden club hitting a sack of sand, thick and real. Sammy didn't say a word, that's what I'll always remember. It was as if there was nothing personal in it. It was just something that had to be done. It was just the rules of the game.

Heard much later. Long after I'd been promoted well away from the streets, that Sammy had gone too far one night and had lost his job. It didn't surprise me. The police service has changed. There's no real place for Neanderthals like him anymore. The funny thing is though, when I was on the streets, and things got hairy as they sometimes did. When I called for help, when I thought that my personal safety was at stake, it was usually Sammy that turned up first, and I was always relieved to see him loping up the road, like some simian avenging angel.

Building a Character

PC Thomas Bishop was killed by one Henry Lock on the 20th September 1877, in the village of Bere Regis in Dorset. Lock struck the unfortunate officer with a piece of flint, after an altercation outside a public house. PC Bishop is, to date, the only Dorset officer to be murdered in the execution of his duty. The slain officer left behind a widow and an eleven year old child. The whole village attended his funeral indicating, on the face of it, that he had been held in high esteem by his community. But what can we really know about the character of PC Bishop? Was he a good husband and father? Was he a diligent officer? Was he the soul of the party, or a quiet man that kept himself to himself? PC Bishop is remembered for the manner of his ending, but a century and a half after his death, we can only know him as a one-dimensional character. Its first-hand experience and memory that paints real characters.

These characters are three dimensional. They're held in my memory, or in the memory of people who have related their tales to me. These anecdotes are real.

PC Larry Devlin, not his real name, was a rough diamond. An ex-serviceman he practiced violence, and in the permissive world of the seventies and eighties, he could do so without real fear of censure. A group of football fans, resplendent with scarfs visited the town where Larry worked, parading down the street singing their favourite songs. Larry, for no apparent reason waded into them, his wooden truncheon swinging to left and right. He arrested a couple of fans who begged to be sent straight back to their city where, they claimed, the police were much gentler.

One day a drunk motorist refused to leave his vehicle when challenged by other officers. He held onto the vehicle's door pillar for dear life and would not be pried off. Larry arrived and his trusty truncheon removed some of the motorist's front teeth before he readily agreed to submit to police requests.

During the eighties miner's strike Larry was performing duty during the cold winter of 1984-85. He was tasked with keeping an eye on a group of pickets outside a Midlands pit. The striking miners had been displaying a large banner between two wooden poles proclaiming, "Victory to the Miners." It was bitingly cold. In an effort to keep warm the strikers had set up a burning brazier in a cut-off oil drum. After a while they decided to go and find some hot tea, driving the two poles into the ground so that their banner could still proclaim their message whilst they sought refreshment. When they returned, they discovered that Larry had rolled up their banner and thrust it into the fire of their brazier. The flames reached high, the wood and canvas of the banner sparked into the dark winter sky, as Larry looked on from across the pit road. I wasn't present, but I can guess at his smile of demented satisfaction.

PC Devlin is real, and is a person who you might describe as a "Character." Every profession has them, but the police force seemed to be an environment that attracted "hyper characters." I say 'seemed to" because I'm not sure that this is the case currently. Maybe it was because of the extreme situations that police found themselves in that allowed such people to indulge in their outlandish behaviour.

Another example is a man that I'll call PC Dave South. He always seemed to have a fixed grin on his face. He could be called upon to perform very accurate Clint Eastwood impressions. In fact, he did them when no one had called upon him to do so. He was prone to patrolling off duty in his own white Ford Granada, the car of choice for traffic policing in the eighties. It was said that he stopped vehicles using a detachable blue light, even reporting his victims for summons. This, universally known and discussed behaviour, didn't seem to bother the senior officers at the time. PC South was eventually sacked, not for his extracurricular activities, but after a domestic disturbance at his police house, when he was alleged to have assaulted his long-suffering wife.

PC Josh Lawrence had a drinking problem in the eighties, a quite severe drinking problem. Brandy was his poison. Josh had an ace in the hole though. He did impressions of the Superintendent in charge of his station. He would perform these to a full bar to the delight of the assembled, and one night the Superintendent appeared unexpectedly, and was also delighted by the mimicry. From then on Josh could do no wrong. He appeared on the BBC programme, "That's Life," with a parrot owned by his father in law, a local licensee. He was asked if he knew of any other police officers with unusual hobbies. He told them that the Superintendent in question was a national gurning champion. Gurning is the ancient art of pulling a grotesque face.

Of course, that Superintendent was not in the habit of entering gurning competitions, so when the BBC researchers called him, to ask if he would appear on their programme, he flew into a rage, which was usual when a matter displeased him. He controlled himself sufficiently to ask why the BBC had got the idea that he did engage in such competitions. The reply prompted him to descend from his office to the policing section offices ranting, "Fucking Lawrence, where is he?" The Sergeant and Inspector were in conference when the irate senior officer burst in, demanding the whereabout of PC Lawrence. By this time, he'd calmed down enough to explain the nub of the situation to the other two officers. Despite his lofty rank the two began to laugh, soon the Superintendent joined in.

Late one night, whilst inebriated, PC Lawrence telephoned the control room, and using the voice of the Superintendent declared, "I'm ordering the instigation of Plan Red," immediately slamming down the receiver. After half an hour of interrogating computer systems and assorted binders, containing contingency plans, the Inspector in charge of the Control Room could find no trace of Plan Red and was becoming very concerned. As a last resort he telephoned the Superintendent, waking him and his wife from their slumbers. When the situation was explained to him the great man bellowed, "That's fucking Lawrence again! I'll fucking kill him." Of course, he didn't, nor take any other action against him, because he had taken a liking to him and his antics. I doubt any other officer, not so favoured, would be likewise indulged.

Then there was PC Knight, as I will call him. I only met him once and he had retired before we could work in the same division together. He was a character. He was a wheeler and dealer. He had his hand in a great many business interests by all accounts, even it was rumoured, in the early seventies fledgling porn industry. Twenty years later a colleague pointed out a flat where such films were allegedly made with the connivance of PC

Knight, in the era of the Burt Reynolds moustache, flared trousers and run-away inflation.

Of course, such entrepreneurial activity was not allowed, as police officers are prohibited from having business interests without the permission of the chief constable. I had to seek permission in the nineties when I made a little money, writing for a police magazine and a local newspaper. PC Knight would not have applied for such permission for his business activities, but his wheeling and dealing was so well known it's impossible that senior officers didn't know about it. That he was allowed to continue, says much about the both the vagaries of rule enforcement, and how selective that enforcement was, dependent on the connections of the individual officer. PC Knight could have been popular with the top brass, or he could have possessed compromising information on them. Who knows?

There's no denying that PC Knight could be described as a character. During the oil crisis, brought about by the Yom Kippur War of 1973, that caused ballooning petrol prices, a 30 mile limit was imposed on each patrol car per shift, in an effort to save expensive fuel. A shift was half over when PC Knight's Sergeant, gazing out of the window, was amazed to see the officer skipping off a bus, before breezing into the station. When asked where his patrol car was, he replied, "In Acacia Road. I've done my 30 miles. During another shift he had not answered his radio for an hour. When he eventually resurfaced and was asked where he'd been, he replied that he was getting his hair cut. "You can't get your hair cut on duty," his irate supervisor told him. "Why not," he replied, "It grows on duty!"

As with PC Lawrence, not all officers could get away with this. But a few did. I don't know if The Job attracts such characters in greater numbers than any other profession. They certainly bring a bit of colour and spice to the workplace.

Sarge, I've Got a Problem

During my first week in the Job, we were sat dutifully amending our Home Office manuals of guidance, when the recruiting Sergeant decided to grace with some pearls of his wisdom. He'd been depressing us all week about how easy it was to drop ourselves in the shit on the streets. We'd reached a point when we all believed that the streets we'd joined to patrol, were a such a minefield of contradictions and unsolvable problems, that we'd all be collecting our P45s within a week of being let out on our own. But this day he imparted to us a gem that would stand us all in good stead, certainly it did me, on that not so distant day that we'd completed training school, served our month with our tutor constable, and had been unleashed, raw and untested on an unsuspecting public.

"Sergeants are the most important people in the police force," he preached, "Just like the army, they run everything that matters. They will be your best friend if you try to do your best, even if you mess up, but do it in good faith. But they will be your worst enemy if you're lazy, or you mess up, then try to pull the wool over their eyes."

Even now, forty years later, I endorse his sentiments wholeheartedly. This was certainly true, on that Monday morning in October 1982, when I reported at 0545hrs for my first ever shift. This remains true to this day, even if the current manifestations of the rank do not, on the whole, appear to live up to this.

In the early eighties most sergeants were men, and most were men, with more than fifteen years service. They were bluff, plain speaking, you didn't want to get on the wrong side of them. My first station sergeant was a man that had been one of the crew of HMS Amethyst, during the famous Yangtse Incident in 1949, when the Royal Navy frigate ran the Chinese Communist blockade to break out into the open sea. A film was made of it, starring Richard Todd, called, "Yangtse Incident." This was the vintage and calibre of these men. I was promoted to sergeant less than seven years later, at the age of thirty. None of my sergeants were that young when I first ventured out on patrol.

There were good ones, and there were bad ones, but the common factor was that you didn't mess around with them. You gave them the respect that they were due, or you knew about it. That's all gone, much to the detriment of the service, and to the public the police serve. In his book "Tango, Juliet Foxtrot," retired Superintendent Ian Donnelley bemoans the loss of the experienced sergeants, recalling that, when he joined in the mid-eighties, most sergeants, "Had somewhere between 15 and 25 years service. So they'd seen it all."

The old police adage, that what gets you in the shit are one of the three Ps. Prisoners, Property or Policewomen. I'm glad to say that the third of this triumvirate caused me no trouble at all, but I've witnessed many a colleague who has not been so fortunate. On one occasion, very early in my service, I fell foul the second of these terrors. I'd entered a motor-cycle, seized by police, onto the property system on behalf of a traffic officer who'd found it, believing it to be stolen. A few months later I received a reminder from the property store, asking me if I still required the bike to be retained. Police property stores are always awash with all kinds of objects, from evidence, like burglary tools, to lost property, like wallets or handbags. I once seized thirty lobster pots, the subject of an allegation of theft by one fisherman against another. The trouble those pots caused me, over a prolonged period of time, could be the subject of a whole book. In the case of this motor-cycle, in my naivety, I replied to the reminder that, this was not my case, and the property store could do what they wanted with it. The bike was sold, just before the owner arrived to claim it. It turned out to be a rare example of its type, and much more valuable than the price police had obtained for it at auction. This episode resulted in a visit for me to the office of the Chief Inspector, who clearly had little time for my defence, that it was all the fault of the traffic officer, as I'd seized the bike on his behalf.

I was very clearly in trouble. One of my Sergeants, a great guy, who wore the oak leaves of the Queen's award for bravery on his tunic, spent an entire afternoon with me, cunningly crafting a written report that downplayed my culpability, refashioning my actions until they sounded noble, indeed in line for commendation. That's how the best sergeants operated. They knew how the system worked, and how to operate it in the interests of their guys.

They were great organisers. When we were chasing burglars, as we did quite often in those days, the sergeant would organise a cordon, skilfully direct officers to contain an area. They really were supervisors in the fullest sense of the word. That does not happen today. One of the best organisers in that respect was also one of the most irascible. One day I had done something minor that irritated him. He had me patrolling a far flung and unusually hilly part of the town for the whole shift, on a heavy black police cycle, that looked like, and handled like, one model up from a penny farthing. I never did find out what my infraction was. But, like most of that vintage, he was a complex character, who would do anything to help any of his men or women if they needed it. He was always the first to ensure the welfare of his staff if they were sick, or had been injured on duty. One day he overheard me telling someone that my car was playing up. He was a bit of an amateur mechanic, and he offered to come and have a look at it. He did the trick and sorted the problem out.

On the whole they weren't graduates, most of them weren't looking on the rank as a stepping stone to greater things. They were sergeants, and that's what they wanted to be. They were bluff men. I've known some that settled disputes with other sergeants with their fists. One big man, long moustache like Australina fast blower Dennis Lillee in his heyday, was a thorn in the side of the Superintendent in charge of the station. The boss, also a man to speak his mind, had to bid farewell to the Sergeant when he was transferred to another station. "I'm glad you're going because I don't fucking like you," was the Superintendents warm message to send the man on his way. "I'm glad I'm going to, because I fucking hate your guts," was the swift reply. At least both knew exactly where they stood.

A PC colleague of mine was completing paperwork, one dark winter's evening, when he heard a commotion. It sounded like furniture was being roughly turned over in the Inspector's office. He hurried to see what was occurring, only to find a Sergeant and an Inspector locked in a tight embrace, clothes dishevelled, chairs and table upended. They were wrestling over some unknown dispute. At least they had the decency to break apart when my colleague walked in on them.

During the miner's strike, we were stood by in a field in Warwickshire, on a balmy summer's afternoon in summer 1984. Rounders was being played with truncheons to pass the time. It was well known amongst us that the two Sergeants of our PSU didn't get on, but no one knew the source of their enmity. One Sergeant struck the ball a good distance and began to run the bases. As he trotted past the other Sergeant he found himself flat on his face, the victim of a leg, left trailing in his path. He sprang to his feet and into the attack, locked in a titanic tussle with his enemy, until we rushed in and prized them apart. The Inspector, sat reading on the steps of one of the vans, pretended not to see the whole sorry incident.

Of course, there were wrong 'uns too. One of my Sergeants in the eighties was a conniving figure, who made Machiavelli look like Florence Nightingale. He would continually undermine the men and women on the squad by gossiping about them behind their backs, or probing people for information that might be of use to him. I was on patrol with him one night when he confided in me that another Sergeant on our squad, who was supposed to be his friend, had the misfortune of having a nervous breakdown some years before. "He'd cried like a baby," he said. Such events were not as sympathetically viewed in those days as they are today. I can only assume that he was prompting me to say something negative about the man, so that he could report back, thus gaining some nebulous advantage. On another occasion, he confided in me that he didn't think that our Inspector was a good organiser, then asked my opinion. By this time, we'd all gotten wise as to this man's character, and were reticent to speak to him unless we had to. I replied that I thought the Inspector was a good man and we were lucky to have him. I'm sure that any other reply would have been immediately reported. To all our relief this man was going places, and after a year of suffering him, he was moved to CID.

Years later, when I was a Sergeant in another town an experienced female officer was posted onto my squad. She had been working as a DC on a regional unit, out of county. After I'd known her for a while, she told me that my erstwhile, conniving Sergeant, had been her Chief Inspector at her last posting. He'd been so disliked that she'd organised her leaving do in secret, so that he couldn't attend. I think he ended up a Superintendent. For sociopaths the end goal is much more important than the good opinion of their staff.

Such men, overwhelmingly good, but also sometimes bad, are long gone. By the time the new century dawned the men and women, who were the new cohort of sergeants were of a completely different breed. The old breed, and my generation of supervisor, were always at work half and hour before the commencement of the shift. A handover from the previous shift was very important, paperwork had to be looked at, beats organised. I shy away from calculating how much of my own time I gave to the Dorset Police over the years. But that's the way it was. I don't regret any of it.

The new sergeants, those I witnessed as I entered my third decade in the Job, turned up at one minute before the commencement of their shift. They acted as more of a senior PC than a sergeant. There was little direction of their, ever dwindling numbers of staff, out on the beat. Poole and Bournemouth boasted five stations in the middle 2000s, down from seven a few years before. As Duty Inspector I did my best to visit each station at least once during my tour of duty. Almost invariably I would find the sergeant at each station sat at their computer, checking incident logs or crime reports, rather than being out with their staff, influencing what was going on out on the streets. Incidentally, today there are only three police stations left out of the original seven in the Poole/Bournemouth conurbation.

The sergeants of thirty years ago were leaders. To be an effective leader there has to be a certain remoteness. A leader should be approachable when guidance is needed, but far enough removed that discipline can be imposed if required. I liked and admired most of the sergeants I worked with early in my career, but they were not my mates, they were my bosses, who could impose the appropriate sanction if required. My observation of sergeants today is that they are the mates of their staff.

I've spoken to people that still work in the service, and they tell me this problem has reached such a pitch, that it is not uncommon for PCs, many very young in service, to argue with their sergeants, even refusing to carry out orders. To question orders that an individual PC considers to be a mistake, with good reason, is healthy. A refusal to carry out an order, provided that the action ordered is lawful, is a serious offence under Police Discipline Regulations.

Ian Donnelley is uncompromising on this issue, "My message to Sergeants is this: the PCs are not your mates. You can be friendly and approachable, when the time comes to give someone a bollocking, you need to be able to do that with confidence. The police is a disciplined service."

In 2017 a young vulnerable woman, Gaia Pope went missing from her Swanage home. Her body was found in undergrowth on a cliff called Dancing Ledge, eleven days later, she had died from hypothermia. Due to her mental health, it was clear that Gaia was vulnerable, and was at very high risk from the very first. On the evening that Gaia went missing the only supervisor on duty was an Acting Sergeant at Wareham, a town ten miles away. An acting sergeant is a PC who performs the duties of a sergeant, but does yet have the skill or experience to be promoted. The PC at Swanage did start to search for Gaia, but, on his own, his effectiveness was limited. The Acting Sergeant did not summon more help, and didn't communicate the urgency of the situation to the night cover Sergeant at Poole, twenty miles away, before going off duty. The Acting Sergeant was subsequently disciplined, but no one else higher up the chain of command suffered any sanction.

In their response to criticism of police conduct from the coroner at the inquest into Gaia's death the Dorset Police stated, "The record of inquest reflects that there were failings on the part of Dorset Police in our response to Gaia's disappearance, but that those failings did not cause or contribute to her death." There were failings on the night that this unfortunate young woman went missing, but they're dwarfed by the failings of the Force management to adequately staff and supervise the area. If there had still been one competent sergeant in place to oversee the policing of the area that evening, things may have turned out very differently.

Without experienced, motivated sergeants, equipped with adequate leadership skills, the police service is in trouble. The Recruiting Sergeants statement decades ago, that the sergeant rank is the most important in the police service, is as true today as it was then.

Custody

There is an earlier version of this chapter. I begin it with a comedy section that reads like an episode of the Sweeney, that popular 70s TV show about the Met's Flying Squad. Flared trousers, spinning of drums (searching houses,) people having it away on their toes (escaping) and crooks engaging in all sorts of villainy. The purpose was to show how easy it was, prior to 1986, for officers, particularly CID officers, to deposit a prisoner in the cells, and just getting around to dealing with them when they felt like it, because of just how unregulated the whole custody procedure was back then.

Then came the Police and Criminal Evidence Act 1984 (PACE) and The Prosecution of Offences Act 1985, the latter setting up the Crown Prosecution Service. I went through the reasons for that, the police failings and the public disquiet at some miscarriages of justice, and how these pieces of legislation bureaucratised a system that had faults, but basically worked well.

But, on reading back through my 1800 words, I realised that I was boring myself, so I would definitely bore any potential reader. Suffice it to say that before the 1st January 1986 the paperwork connected with arrested persons was minimal, allowing the police to get on and do their job protecting the public. After that date the demands of PACE, and the Codes of Practice made under its auspices, and, additionally of the newly minted Crown Prosecution Service, ensured that police officers have been snared in a net of bureaucracy ever since. More time spent at a desk writing, or now, tapping on a computer, is less time out of the streets protecting the public.

But, what of custody? When it seemed certain that I was going to be promoted to sergeant, in the late eighties, I was posted to the cells as gaoler, the assistant to the sergeant custody officer, so that I could learn the ropes. The gaoler, all police officers in those days, now all civilians, documented property, checked the prisoners hourly, weighing in when any physical restraint was necessary.

On my promotion I was posted to Wareham, a small station with one cell and a juvenile detention room. In those days, if it seemed that a prisoner could be dealt with quickly, he, and it was nearly always he in those days, could be booked in and dealt with at Wareham. I was particularly grateful to two members of my squad, who were very keen on winkling out drivers who had been over imbibing, and were over the drink drive limit. Drunk drivers couldn't be released until they blew a negative test on the breathalyser. If it seemed that this would happen in the early hours I kept them at Wareham, charging and bailing them, thus earning some much needed overtime. If they were heavily intoxicated, off they went to permanent custody centres, at Poole or Weymouth, for an overnight stay.

Poole and Bournemouth are two towns, but are in actuality, one quite heavily populated single urban area. In those days both had a custody block, or suite as it became known. For a time in the eighties Bournemouth was the busiest custody suite in the whole country. Poole could also be very hectic and, after less than two years at Wareham, I found myself there, as a permanent custody officer in, what was, my home-town.

Poole custody suite has long since passed into history, that station being forfeited in a Private Finance Initiative deal in around 2010. It's now a block of flats. But then, in 1990, it had sixteen cells, and life there could be very demanding. The custody sergeant is the boss in the block. I really enjoyed the responsibilities. Handling sixteen prisoners at a time was sometimes quite a task. That was sixteen sets of circumstances, sixteen risk profiles, as when a person comes into custody, their safety is the responsibility of the custody officer alone.

On busy nights you might have a DC waiting to explain why his detainee should be charged with GBH with intent, (Section 18 of the Offences Against the Person Act 1861,) while you're booking in a man for a public order offence, who looks like he's about to become violent, against the background noise of someone kicking their cell door, mingling with blood curdling screams from another cell, while other prisoners, who just want to go to sleep, are threatening violence if the miscreants don't shut up. There could well be three other prisoners sat in police vehicles outside, waiting to come before you, to be booked in. At the time, I was thirty-two, and found the whole thing exhilarating, feeling an enormous sense of satisfaction driving home after a busy shift. Now, in my mid-sixties, those memories just makes me feel very weary, wondering how I did it.

The custody officer's worse fear is the death of a prisoner in custody. When this happens every aspect of the deceased treatment and care while in the care of the custody officer, will be pored over with a fine-toothed comb. This is, of course, what should happen. As I've said everything that happens in that custody block is the responsibility of the custody officer. The PACE Act is supplemented by Codes of Practice, that govern the treatment and welfare of detainees, their questioning, identification and many other things besides. When they were first published, in 1986, they were the size of a slim airport novel. Peter Hitchens described the Act as seeming "To have been devised by left wing lawyers *for* left wing lawyers." Today, these codes of practice are not the size of the Encyclopaedia Britannica, but not far short. If one person is responsible for the processing, welfare, safety, charging and bailing of sixteen individual prisoners, with all the vagaries of their medical needs, vulnerabilities, even their dietary requirements, it's very easy for a great many of these needs to pass under the radar.

I was lucky enough, and it was luck, to get away without a death in custody on my watch. It did happen while I was there in 1990 to 1993, but not to me. I did come close, however. In 1993 I had authorised the charge of a man who had murdered his wife with a hammer. It was a very disturbing case. There appeared to be no motive, just out of the blue, he had killed her whilst she had been reading, in bed before going to sleep. He was quite clearly a suicide risk. I'd filled in an "Exceptional Risk" form that detailed these concerns. This form would accompany him to court, being passed on to the prison service, so that they'd been aware during his remand, taking measures to negate the risk, or they should have done.

Sure enough, he did commit suicide in Winchester Prison while remanded. A few months later I received a concerning phone call from a DS, who had attended the inquest into the death of the murderer. He told me that the prison service had claimed, giving evidence at the inquest, that no Exceptional Risk form had been passed to them, they were therefore unaware of the potential for suicide. I knew that a copy of the form, that I'd personally completed, was securely attached to the man's custody record, safely filed away in Dorset Police records. If this hadn't been the case, I could have been in very hot water. It's very easy to fall foul of a bureaucracy that's always looking for scapegoats, and is populated by dishonourable people, looking for ways to avoid their responsibilities.

In those days the custody officer authorised charges. The investigating officer presented the evidence, the custody officer decided if that evidence justified the criteria for charge. The system worked well. I authorised the charges for some very serious offences including murder. If a system works well, it won't be long before someone feels the need to change it. In the latter years of the 2010s the custody officer was relieved of this responsibility. The authority to charge, and to authorise a remand in custody, was given to a CPS prosecutor. Clearly, such a learned council is not available 24 hours a day, as the custody officer always is. Prosecutors would hold "clinics" at intervals, in office hours, where investigating officer would queue to have five minutes with them. At other times there would be a duty prosecutor, who might be in any part of the country, perhaps hundreds of miles away from where the offence took place. An investigating officer would have to email, or fax the relevant statements to that prosecutor, before they would make any decision. Often prosecutors would not be contactable, thereby necessitating the bailing of a suspect to come back to the police station at a later date, even if there was more than sufficient evidence to charge him. This slowed the system down for the benefit of no one, victim, offender, or hard-pressed investigating officer.

The huge increase in the use of bail before charge, known as 47(3) bail, came to the attention of the new Home Secretary, Theresa May, when she assumed the post in 2010. Before I describe her intervention as regards 47(3) bail I must put my cards on the table. In my opinion Ms May was, by far, the worst Home Secretary in my time in the Job. That is quite a statement when you consider that this span covers the time in office of David Blunkett, Kenneth Clarke and Jacqui Smith amongst others. May was the only Home Secretary, with perhaps the possible exception of Clarke, to be openly anti police. She presided with glee over a 20% cut in the police budget, cuts that so wounded the service, that it has still to recover. Her speech, to the Police Federation Conference in 2015, was dripping with contempt for the men and women that put on the uniform each day, risking their safety for the sake of the public. She described the Federation's warning, that cuts were endangering public safety, as "scaremongering." Well, time has proven her very wrong, but, as with all politicians, she has paid no price for it, now sitting comfortably in her ermine in the House of Lords, as Baroness May, of Maidenhead. Her cack-handed time at the Home Office, added to her subsequent car crash as Prime Minister, proving the adage that people in high office always fail upwards.

As part of her bad mouthing of the police, Mrs May chided the service for bailing too many offenders before charge, calling for a drastic cut in those numbers. In response the police introduced a system called "released under investigation," in which a person is simply released, with no specified date to return, and no conditions that safeguards victims, or witnesses.

After my retirement, in 2018, I was working for Bournemouth Borough Council as an anti-social behaviour officer. A man had broken into a council property, assaulted an occupant with an iron bar, breaking his arm, then proceeding on a rampage of damage with an axe. To arrest him the police found it necessary to deploy a Taser. I contacted Bournemouth Police, to enquire as to his bail address, as I wished to serve an injunction on him to bar him from all council property. The police response to my enquiry shocked me. I was told that the man had not been bailed, but released under investigation, a practice that I hadn't heard of until that day. But I was doubly shocked to find out that he had been released without furnishing any fixed address, so that he could be recontacted, or rearrested if thought necessary.

If this was a common occurrence, and I was told it was, then there is no doubt that this puts the public in severe danger from violent offenders, over which the police have no control at all. If this incident had happened when I was a custody officer, this man would have been charged with grievous bodily harm and criminal damage, on my say so. He would then have been kept in custody for the next available court, on the grounds that he posed a danger to victims and witnesses, and because he was also a flight risk, as he had no fixed abode. The court would have been asked for a remand in custody, or bail with strict conditions.

Politicians and senior officers have waxed lyrical over the decades about reducing police bureaucracy, to allow officers the freedom to be visible on the streets to deter crime. It's obvious to me that, despite fine words, the bureaucratic load on an officer has never been heavier.

In 1998 I was promoted to inspector. The inspector rank also has a number of functions within the custody set up. The authorisation of forensic samples, giving permission for the temporary withholding of the detainees right to have someone informed of their arrest, and a number of others. An inspector must enquire, when a person has been in custody for six hours, if their continued custody is justified, then once again nine hours later, noting on the custody record that this has been done. Since the early nineties, when I began to perform acting inspector duties, up until my retirement in 2012, I must have carried out hundreds, if not thousands of reviews, as this function is called. Again, in my opinion, this is unnecessary bureaucracy, as in those twenty years, not once did I ever find that a detained person's custody was not justified. Not once. So, what was the point of all that formulaic word play and form filling? It certainly gives the legal profession a marvellous opportunity to find some minor infraction of PACE, or the codes of practice, to amplify in court, to muddy the waters, to obfuscate the true facts of the case.

Of course, the police have the responsibility for ensuring a person's safety and fair treatment while they are in custody. To that end, the risk assessment that a custody officer must complete when a person is booked into custody is extensive, it includes questioning the detainee on his state of mind and his mental health.

Towards the end of my service, I was in a custody block, sat behind the custody desk writing my record of reviews on the custody records. The charge room was full of people performing various tasks. The night before a man had stabbed his girlfriend, thankfully she survived, and he'd then driven his car over a low cliff, presumably in an attempt to kill himself. Miraculously, his injuries were fairly minor. On leaving hospital he'd been arrested on suspicion of wounding, and brought to the custody suite. He was in the process of being booked in, as I sat behind the Custody Sergeant contributing my offering to the paper mountain. The man's detention had been authorized, and his property documented. I started to listen as the Sergeant went through the questions that made up the risk assessment. He asked about any current injuries or medication that might be needed. He then asked,

"Have you had any suicidal thoughts or tried to harm yourself in the last forty-eight hours?" There was a slight pause, then he added, "Apart from driving your car over the cliff last night, I mean." There was a burst of very unprofessional laughter from everyone in the room, including me. Even the girlfriend stabber smiled.

"The Last Great Unreformed Public Sector Union."

When David Cameron began presiding over the new coalition government in May 2010, the country was apparently broke. Outgoing Treasury Secretary Liam Byrne's infamous note, left in a drawer for his successor declaring, "There's no money left," set the tone for the years of austerity that followed. With expenditure on UK police forces, in the financial year 2010-11, adding up to £18 billion, the service was an obvious target for cuts.

From 2001, until I retired in 2012, I was an elected Police Federation Representative on the Inspector's Branch Board. Many uninformed persons refer to the Police Federation as "the police trade union." It was clear that the government saw the police service as ripe for reform. The Police Federation were seen as an obstacle to that reform. The Home Affairs Select Committee of Parliament, pronounced that there was "Overwhelming evidence of the need for the Federation, whose structure and operation have changed little in the century since its inception, to change and reform." Home Secretary Theresa May, stormed into the Police Federation Conference in Bournemouth in 2015 telling delegates, in a speech that stunned the hall, that she was going to reform the police and break the power of the Federation. David Cameron himself described the police as, "The last great unreformed public service." Good stuff, eh? Break union power, get value for our buck? But, like most pictures painted by tricky politicians, the reality was quite different.

In late 2010 at a Dorset Police Federation Meeting, a member related how he'd attended the surgery of his local MP to discuss the negative spin coming from the government on the police service. The MP, typical lobby fodder blustered, "We must crack down on the Spanish Practices enjoyed by police." "Spanish Practices" is a phrase that refers to restrictive procedures, that work in the interests of the workers in a particular trade or profession. When asked by the representative to name one of these, so called, Spanish Practices, the MP could not do so, it was merely waffle and bluster. This confusion and ignorance is typical of politicians, on a glaringly wide spectrum of issues that they are entrusted with adjudicating.

In fact the Police Federation is not a trade union in any accepted sense. A police union had been set up in 1910, in response to poor pay and bad conditions suffered by officers in the opening decade of the century. This new organisation was not recognised by any Chief Constable. During the Great War police conditions of service worsened. Officers were more poorly paid than shop girls, and under wartime conditions, they were forced to work long periods of overtime with no compensation, either in time off, or in payment. Even their one rest day a week, only secured a few years before the war, was suspended. If an officer left the force, to take up a well paid job in the munitions industry, they were immediately drafted into the army for service on the Western Front.

Matters came to a head in August 1918, when officers in the Metropolitan Police came out on strike. Lloyd George's government was forced to capitulate, promising union recognition when the war ended. When hostilities ceased this promise was soon reneged on. Instead, the government appointed Lord Desborough to enquire into police pay and conditions. Desborough's Commission reported in July 1919, recommending hefty pay rises, along with the setting up of a Police Federation, for officers up to the rank of chief inspector. This new body would be split into three branch boards, one each for constables, sergeants and inspectors, including chief inspectors. There would be no right to strike, and a mechanism for settling pay and conditions was imposed. Police unions were banned.

The government hurried through the Police Bill that contained all the recommendations of the Desborough Commission, becoming law on the 30th July 1919. The police union called a strike by end of the month, but only around a thousand Metropolitan officers responded. The strike call was greeted more enthusiastically in Liverpool, where half the force walked out, prompting a mob to roam the streets, engaging in gleeful looting. The government hastily despatched a battleship, HMS Valiant, and two destroyers up the Mersey, with a complement of Royal Marines, to restore order. The strike collapsed. Every single striker was dismissed from both the Metropolitan Police and the Liverpool Force.

The basic arrangements that govern the Police Federation, from its inception in 1919, persist to the present day. All rules, from elections, to the arrangements of conferences, and the composition of branch boards, are governed by act of parliament. A powerful, unreformed public service union? I think not.

The vast majority of Federation work is carried out at the local level, representing officers that have fallen foul of discipline regulations, have a grievance, after being treated unfairly, or need legal representation when accused of breaching the criminal law. Incidentally, the bill for this legal representation is paid for by members subscriptions, not by the taxpayer, as many mistakenly assume.

Whilst a Federation representative I took on responsibility for organising an annual holiday for officers of the Royal Ulster Constabulary, who had been injured by terrorist action during the troubles. A local seaside hotel donated a room for the officer and his or her family. The RUC Federation paid for the flights from Ulster, the Dorset Police provided a car, and Dorset Federation representatives acted as guides in their own time.

I was an equality representative, meaning I advised officers who alleged that they'd been ill treated by the Force on matters related to policy. On one occasion officers had lost their positions on CID, but the Force had not followed their own transfer policy. This was, and probably still is, a common occurrences. When senior officers trumpet a marvellous new policy, then fail to follow it. All the officers were reinstated on CID.

I represented an officer who had been stripped of his grade for promotion to sergeant. I argued his case before the Superintendent, who had been appointed to investigate his grievance. But sometimes in those situations you argue from a very weak position. The officer worked at a rural station. One night he was sent with a colleague to a report of a rape at a music festival. His handling of the case was so cack-handed, indeed downright incompetent, that I was forced to agree with the

Superintendent that this officer was unlikely to measure up as a sergeant at the current time. This highlights a problem experienced by officers at rural stations. They simply do not deal with the breadth and volume of serious incidents that allow them to become proficient, as officers in busy urban stations do.

Most forces allow officers to take a career break of a year, or even longer. This is intended to refresh them, see the world from a new perspective, to come back with a new enthusiasm for their police career. That's the theory. Officers on career break are not supposed to take paid employment during this sabbatical, but many do, a blind eye is often turned to it. Not many people can live for a year without income.

During the first decade of this century the Caribbean country of Trinidad and Tobago decided to invest some of its wealth, obtained from exploitation of its oil and gas resources, into improving its police force. The country has experienced an upsurge in violent crime since the 1990s, mostly fuelled by the drug trade. The number of murders in the country jumped from 98 in 1998 to 550 in 2008. It was found that T & T officers could not perform basic tasks, such as statement taking. De-escalation of confrontational situations by officers was not common, leading to frequent fatal police shootings, deaths in custody and numerous reports of police brutality. In 2006 a UNHCR report told a story of police brutality and unlawful killings by the Island's police, calling for wide scale reforms.

Partly in response to this report, lucrative contracts were awarded to companies, in large part set up by former British police officers, to retrain and modernise Trinidadian police. Many of these companies employed those British police officers who were on a career break. Later, acting on legal advice, the Association of Chief Police Officers instructed that all serving British Police officers should be recalled from their contracts in Trinidad. Trinidad still employed the death penalty, and still does. Police chiefs were concerned that, if a British police officer should be involved in an investigation that resulted in the imposition and carrying out of sentence of death, this may make this officer, and his or her's force, liable under human rights legislation.

I was passed a case that had been languishing in the in tray of another Federation rep' for some time. The case concerned an officer that was working in Trinidad on a career break. He had been instructed by the Chief Constable to return to duty in Dorset, an eventuality covered by the appropriate career break policy. The officer seems to have ignored this order, continuing to work on the Island. There wasn't much I could do in the circumstances but point out the inevitable conclusion if he continued to ignore the Chief's express will. This I did repeatedly by way of email. He continued to obfuscate, and, was duly sacked. You can try, but some people you just can't help. Incidentally, The total number of murders in Trinidad climbed to 605 in 2022, with a detection rate of only 12%. Retraining doesn't seem to be having the desired effect.

Tony Judge dedicated his whole working life to the Police Federation, writing the definitive history of the Federation, which was published in 1994. In the foreword to that work he said,

"A lot of nonsense is spoken today about 'police culture.' The police service.... is a very special vocation and at its best, its comradeship and fierce professional pride serve police and people very well. The Federation, while fiercely defending the rights of its members and constantly striving to improve their status, has never lost sight of the principles which make the service truly special."

Judge titled his history, "The Force of Persuasion." He did this because that's all the Federation can do to promote favourable terms and conditions for its members. Police officers have no right to strike, or work to rule, or to encourage other officers to do so. If they do, they commit a criminal offence and will serve prison time. The Federation can only attempt to persuade those in power by force of logical argument.

So, when self-serving politicians try to hoodwink you, into believing that the Police Federation is a radical union, capable of the worst excesses of the bad old days of union power, you will know better.

His Bag (Fiction)

He watched the news at ten, then hefted his canvas bag in the dark hallway. His wife had surveyed him going out, her eyes moving, flickering in the TV light, her head turned pointedly to the telly. He hoped that he'd get out of the door before she said anything. The last thing he needed was her giving him a bloody lecture. Grabbing his green army smock, he eased the front door closed behind him. In the darkness of the porch, he pulled on his smock, and tested the bag. It felt right, the weight was reassuring to him. He knew he had the right tools for the job. He pulled the long strap onto his shoulder, setting off into the Sunday winter darkness.

The main item on the news had made him uneasy. Vans full of coppers travelling in convoy around the country. He hated coppers. He felt sorry for the miners, not because they would lose their jobs if they lost the strike, but because they were stupid enough to have got into that position in the first place. Working for someone else, the only person that you should work for is yourself. His Father had taught him that. As he walked towards town, images of Thatcher passed through his mind. She frightened him, but she excited him too. She took no shit. He felt he was like that, a man that knew where he was going. Mrs T would surely do for those poor sap miners.

The sight of the convoys of police had made him uncomfortable. All those rozzers, all working together to fuck up the miners. There was something that made him feel uneasy in that, all that joined up direction and purpose. But then he thought, that's good for me. If they were all up North giving miners a hard time, there'd be less of 'em at home patrolling his town.

The clinkers on the masts of the yachts at the marina, vibrating in the light wind, serenading him, as he headed further into town. Each boat in a neat row. In the summer he'd stand on the dockside watching those yachties, their branded wind cheaters and fifty quid deck shoes. He had the feeling that they were buying into an image of life that wasn't real. They'd go for drinks in the new wine bars, that he wouldn't be seen dead in, mixing with the same sort of losers. He searched for the word. Phoneys, that's what they were, yes, phoneys. They were just pretending to be something. On Mondays they'd go back to their jobs, skivvying for someone else. He hated them nearly as much as he hated coppers.

The light was orange now. He knew he had to be careful, most people had long since gone home, but you never knew when a copper would appear out of the darkness. He'd done this a hundred times. True, he'd been caught a few times, done time in the nick. But he knew that he was ahead, Never done a days work for another man. Never got up in the morning when he didn't want to. Never had to bow and scrape to any man.

The alley, from Park Row into King Street, was as dark as he wanted it to be. He remembered larking here when he was a kid. Knocking on doors, then disappearing into its gloom. Thieving from the late shop on the corner. This was our home town. No one knew it better than us. We took a few whacks when we were caught. Dad would give me another when I got home, for not getting away with it. That was when he wasn't locked up himself.

The bus station was half-way up King Street. He waited in the dark of the alley. A car droned by at the top of the road, across the seafront. There was no other sound. He was out in the street, walking fast, the buses parked in neat rows, red monsters, parading at rest.

His target was the office, a grey block, single storey building with lots of tempting windows. Windows with no locks. He hoped he'd find one open, but if he didn't, he had his bag. A bus driver had told him that on Fridays they didn't night safe the cash, everyone just wanting to get home for the weekend. They kept it hidden in the office. For the information on where that hiding place was, the driver would get £20. That was fair.

He looked around. He was gratified that a low mist had begun to form. It all seemed to be going his way. He crept around the building trying each window, None gave way to his pushing and pulling.

He'd been keeping a good look out, so he didn't know where they could have come from. But there they were. Two fucking great coppers, in those great coats they wore, with those fucking stupid helmets. They had a sort of resigned, but amused look on their well shaved faces. They were young, and he suddenly felt very old, out of his depth.

"What are you up to, then?" the taller, better built of the two asked. He was sure that this lad must play rugby. The idea of fighting his way out of this was only a passing shadow in his mind.

"I was just looking for somewhere to sleep, I'm homeless." He knew that this was a forlorn strategy. He was well known in the town as a prolific burglar.

The big one again. "Oh, yes. Is that so? What's in the bag?"

"Nothing. Just my odds and ends."

The big one grabbed the bag, but he held onto it, like it was the ball in a rolling maul.

"Why don't you want to give me the bag?" He had a smile on his face, as if he knew all his secrets.

"Because if you see inside this bag, you'll nick me," he said, before he had time to think, his subconscious spilling out of him as if he was a broken vessel.

The big man ripped the bag from his grip. The zip made a strange tearing sound as it opened. He looked on, feeling empty, feeling not of this world. A car drove by making the mist eddy and swirl. The big copper looked up from the jemmies, screwdrivers, other tools lying snug in the bag. He laughed, showing the other the contraband.

"You're right. You're nicked." And he laughed again.

Going equipped to steal was the charge. It would breach his suspended sentence. He was probably going back to prison. He avoided his wife's eyes, as he found her standing in the hallway, as he pushed open the front door in the uncertain light of the following morning. He made himself a coffee, then went out into the back garden, smoking a cigarette, as the sun disappeared behind a cloud, a cold wind blew the stunted brown trees into a swirling dance.

After they'd booked him into custody the two coppers had talked to him as if he was an old friend, that they'd come upon unexpectedly in a seaside pub. They'd photographed him and taken four sets of fingerprints. He remembered the procedure, it was very ordered. A sequence laid down and followed to the letter. It was reassuring somehow that he knew the way that it would go. As the first light greyed the cell window he was charged and bailed. No one needed to tell him what was happening.

"You don't recognise me?" He'd asked the officers as they'd inked his hands, rolled his palms in black.

"No. We're not from this town. We're only here to cover for those guys up North, working on the pit strike. We were going to be day off, but you can't turn down overtime, can you?

"I Never See a Copper Around Here Anymore"

I'm going to attempt to tell you now, how and why police management gave up on a practice that had worked so spectacularly well, keeping the public safe for a century and a half. The practice of police patrol, particularly foot patrol. There are two stories here. They are both about the liberalising zeal of the sixties. When any change was seen as good, the exciting new should always be preferred to the stuffy old. The time of the Beatles, the sexual revolution, women's liberation and swinging London. The first story came about due to a lack of police manpower. The second arose from a belief in an illusion, an illusion that promised that large organisations are more efficient than small ones.

The cliche that heads this chapter. "Never see a policeman walking around here," used to be greeted by the grizzled old bobby, before the early nineties with, "Well, you don't sit in your window looking out all day and night, do you?" If that grizzled old stager was still around today, even he would be forced to admit that, in most cities, villages and towns around the country, patrolling police officers are as rare as rocking horse shit, as the saying goes. To find out why this is the case it's necessary to go back deep into the twentieth century.

The Royal Commission on policing of 1929 stated that,

"The duties of the police may be regarded as falling under three heads. First, the *prevention* (their emphasis) of crimes and offences, rightly regarded by the Police themselves, as their most important duty."

The main buttress of this work of prevention was patrolling, foot patrolling. This truism was taken as unassailable wisdom until after World War Two. In the post war world, recruitment to the police was difficult. The country experienced a "baby boom" from 1945, and again from the mid-fifties. New towns were being built, the old decaying slums of the inner city were being cleared, people moving to shiny new estates on the edges of town, and even brand new towns, such as Hemel Hempstead in Hertfordshire. My own home-town, Poole, began to clear the old substandard housing in the old town, building new council estates on the heaths that ringed the town. In 1962, my family lived in a crumbling old house, without a bathroom, with an outside toilet at the end of the yard. The rooms were bitterly cold and damp in winter. In 1961 the council compulsorily purchased the property from my family's landlord, moving us to a relatively new house on a council estate, with the luxury of an inside bathroom and toilet. All these new estates and towns required policing.

Here I must pause and introduce Eric St Johnson. St Johnson was a Cambridge graduate, Chief Constable of Oxfordshire, then Durham, before becoming the Chief of one of the largest forces in the country, Lancashire, in 1950. He held this post until 1967, when he was elevated to become Chief Inspector of Constabulary.

St Johnson was an enigma. As a man of his time, he held very traditional views. When the Lancashire force cooperated with the production of the television drama "Z cars," that first aired in 1962, St Johnson complained to the BBC that they had "portrayed the wife of a policeman as a slut with a dirty face, and hair in disarray, who ate in a most uncouth manner, using mugs, not cups and saucers, on the table." This in a time when an officer's wife was as much a member of the force as her husband, often answering the telephone on his behalf, or manning a desk in a police house that doubled as a mini station, particularly in rural areas.

But this man, born at the dawn of the twentieth century, was also a fervent moderniser. Lancashire became the first force to introduce radar speed checks in 1957. In 1961 St Johnson purchased ten sets of transistorised transmitters from the Motorola company of Chicago. He wanted to equip each of his patrol officers with personal radio communications. Prior to this, officers relied for information and direction on police telephone boxes, located at various points on their beat. The Motorola radios proved to be too bulky and heavy for such use, so St Johnson instructed the Force radio technicians to develop a lighter set. This they did, the set being commercially produced by the General Electric Company. Lancashire became the first force in the world to equip their officers with such technology, winning awards for this innovation.

In his autobiography, "One Policeman's Story," St Johnson describes the Lancashire force's dilemma. Having to police the new towns, when manpower and recruitment were areas of real difficulty. Kirby, on the outskirts of Liverpool, was one such new town. It had been developed to provide homes for those displaced by slum clearance in Liverpool immediately after the war. The land on which the town stood was purchased for development from the Earl of Sefton in 1947. The town was typical of many urban developments of the time, rushed, with little thought given to social amenities. Although the first occupants were in place by 1952, the first shop didn't open until 1955, the first pub pulling its inaugural pint in 1959.

In response to this problem of resources, St Johnson and his senior officers, proposed a new method of policing, moving the patrolling constable away from their foot beats, a tactic that had served police forces well since the first Metropolitan police officers ventured out from their stations in 1829, to motorised patrol. St Johnson proposed that Kirby would be patrolled by five officers in cars, rather than on foot, on the eleven foot patrol beats. Foot patrols would be confined to the shopping precincts. This new way of patrolling began in May 1965.

St Johnson himself admitted that this was not an ideal situation. "If only we could have a policeman on his feet in every street in every town, the amount of crime and public disorder would be minimal." This is clearly a truism. He goes on to state that car patrol is inimical to public engagement. "The fact remains that once policemen are taken off their feet and put into motor cars, they do lose touch with the public." This method of policing, mostly in vehicles, but supplemented by foot patrols in town centres, became known as, "Unit Beat Policing."

One method by which St Johnson attempted to proclaim that police in cars were still very much present, and visible in the community, was also borrowed from the United States. During a visit to the that country he noticed that many police departments had painted the doors of the vehicles white, with the name of the department conspicuously painted on those doors. Prior to this most police cars in England were a sober dark blue or black. St

Johnson adopted the US colour scheme, instructing that the white door paint should be continued over the top of the car, the rest of the car being sprayed light blue. When these instructions were conveyed to the mechanics in the Lancashire vehicle workshops, one of them, wiping his hands on his oily rag, was heard to comment, "Have you heard the latest mad idea of the Chief? He wants the Kirby cars to look like bloody pandas." The name stuck. When I joined the Job in 1982, the three mobile patrol areas in Weymouth, were known as "panda areas."

The Police Advisory Board met on the 7th December 1966, under the chairmanship of the Home Secretary, Roy Jenkins. Peter Hitchens in his book, "A Brief History of Crime," dubs this meeting as, "One of the most revolutionary gatherings in post war British politics." The Board proclaimed that all chief constables should adopt the "reshaping of the beat system." That meant "Unit Beat Policing."

In August 1967 the Home Office issued a circular reiterating this message. Central government not only encouraged UBP, described by the Chief Inspector of Constabulary in his annual report as, "The biggest change in fundamental operational policing methods since 1829," but they were willing find the money to pay for the extra vehicles, radios and other technical support, that this change demanded. Forces eagerly accepted this, unusual, largesse from central government.

A Home Office working party report, published by HMSO in January 1967, upon which the decision of the Police Advisory Board was based, still asserted that the old beat system still worked well, "By his mere presence the uniform policeman undoubtedly prevents some crime and affords a degree of protection to life and property." It also concedes that a uniform officer on foot patrol, is the means by which, "The concept of a citizen in uniform gains reality." But with this conceded the adoption of UBP still went full speed ahead.

This Damascene conversion to the virtues of Unit Beat Policing, although covered by the fig leaf of "research," was really a response to a massive recruitment and retention crisis in the police. On January 1st 1966 police forces in England and Wales were 7,846 officers under strength. That was 11% below the number authorised by the Home Office. One in six forces were 20% understrength.

But, just a year later, the idea that a policeman on foot was the ideal, and Unit Beat Policing was merely a response to low manpower, had been swept away. A 1968 Central Office of Information film, extolling the virtues of UBP, shows officers in brand new Ford Anglia patrol vehicles, working closely with those officers still left on foot patrol in a cold northern winter. An avuncular Director of the Police Research and Development Branch explains that 2 years of "research" had concluded that the traditional constable on foot patrol beat, "Does no positive work against crime." A statement at variance with all official pronouncements up to that time, and an idea that would have surprised most uniform constables, working hard on their beats since 1829. The Director went on to proclaim that, "One conspicuous patrol car will do the work of at least five uniform foot patrols, when it comes to prevention." The research that informed this film must have been what we used to call "foregone conclusion research." In other words, "Here is the result that we want you to achieve, find some research to back it up." If not, how could any research conclude that five foot patrols, equals the work of one mobile patrol. Cars come and go, the driver is driving, his attention is diverted from his surroundings by the mechanical act of operating the motor car. A constable on foot patrol can focus his total attention on his surroundings. There is no metal skin insulating him from contact with Mrs Coombes, the sub post mistress, or Mr Ralph, digging away on his allotment, or Fred the local burglar, moving furtively away into the back alley when he catches sight of the blue uniform.

In her much cited 1986 book, Innovations in Policing," Mollie Weatheritt, a former Assistant Director of the Police Foundation, described the "research" referred to by the Director of the Police Research and Development Branch as, "Thin and oversold," and the evidence that Unit Beat Policing was an improvement on the traditional method of policing as a, "Mythology."

The Home Office was also eager to trumpet this new policing methods as improving the job satisfaction of constables. They would, "Elevate the status of the beat constable in a way that would bring out the best qualities of a policeman." This would help to solve the problem of recruitment. This proved to be another myth, as the high inflation and economic stagnation of the seventies, further eroded the attractiveness of the police as a career, as police pay lagged behind other professions, such as the coal miners, who had the union muscle to bully the government into large, inflation matching, pay rises. It wasn't until the Edmund Davies pay review, recommending a 45% pay increase to officers, was fully implemented by the Thatcher Government in 1979, that forces began to recruit up to their establishment levels. I was one of those young men and women, who were washed into policing on the tide of the Edmund Davies award.

For a supposed scientific approach to policing, Unit Beat Policing remained remarkably free of any formal evaluation. As Mollie Weatheritt points out, the 1967 Police Research and Planning Report, by Superintendent E. Gregory, most cited as such an evaluation, is nothing of the sort. She describes it as "More of an operational *aide memoire,* providing helpful hints for forces thinking about implementing unit beat policing." Therefore, the extravagant claims made by the proponents of the new policing remained unverified.

Disillusionment soon set in. In her 1983 book, "The Policing Revolution. Police, Technology, Democracy and Liberty in Britain," Sarah Mainwaring White observed,

"The pandas were, it is widely agreed, a disaster. They distanced the police from the public and, it has been suggested, encouraged policemen to see themselves as knights-errant in the war against crime rather than members of the community."

But if Unit Beat Policing had been an attempt to address the inability of forces to provide sufficient resources to patrol on foot in the traditional way, at least it was a good faith attempt. Amalgamation of forces had a more dubious bloodline. UBP inadvertently destroyed the service's dedication to preventive foot patrol, with disastrous results. Amalgamation made forces into oversized behemoths, insulating decision makers from what actually occurs on the streets, fostering a culture of sterile managerialism, a remoteness from the consequences of operational decisions.

My experience of policing in the 80s, in my small South Coast, medium sized town, was that our version of Unit Beat

Policing worked fairly well. We would typically parade ten or twelve officers, two sergeants and an inspector. With three panda areas, this left at least seven officers to patrol on foot, more than enough slack to allow officers catch up with paperwork, or to deal with prisoners in the cells. I'd never experienced an era when foot patrol was the only show in town. In my view the combination of foot and panda cars worked well. But already there was a spectre, invisible to my inexperienced eye, but slowly, inexorably, taking shape just over the horizon.

In 1984 criminologists Ronald Clarke and Mike Hough produced a report for the Home Office Research and planning unit with the title, "Crime and Police Effectiveness." The report evaluated differing methods of addressing crime, from specialist teams to community policing. But it was one comment, on routine foot patrol, that would be the report's main contribution to the demise of this most traditional of policing methods.

"The chance that a (foot) patrol would catch an offender in the act is remote. A patrol officer in London could expect to pass within 100 yards of a burglary only once every 8 years, but might not even realise that the crime was taking place."

Leaving aside as to how this dubious statistic was arrived at, the point hardly worth making is that the primary objective of foot patrol is prevention of crime and disorder, with detection a distant secondary.

Routine Activity Theory again. If the burglar believes that there is a capable guardian nearby, in all likelihood he will not attempt the burglary. If he knows that the local police have completely given up on patrolling, he will feel emboldened to do what he wants.

On the 2nd November 2019 a gang of burglars broke into a jewellers in the small seaside town of Swanage in Dorset. This was no clandestine crime as locals in a pub opposite came out, pints in hand, to watch, and even film what was taking place. The Bournemouth Echo describes the scene,

"Members of the gang took their time to break into the Georgian Gems jewellers in the High Street while about 20 (pub) customers gathered to watch yards away."

When I was promoted to sergeant, in 1989, I was posted to Wareham, police station. Wareham is a small town in the beautiful Purbeck Hills, Swanage, the scene of the burglary is ten miles away through those hills, sitting in its Victorian splendour on the rocky coast. In those days both Wareham and Swanage police could boast three sergeants apiece, along with twenty-four hour patrols. In 1989 there would have been at least three officers on patrol in Swanage in the early evening, the time of the jewell burglary 30 years later. Through the 1990s and 2000s, the number of staff working in the Purbecks declined. Swanage police station was closed in 2013, the holiday resort being covered from Wareham police station, ten miles away. A local commented on social media in 2019.

"Criminals are realising that the police presence in Swanage is so bad they can literally rob a shop in a busy town and the police won't turn up for 20-30 minutes."

The criminal mindset is simple. If I stand no chance of the police being in the area, and I face no chance of apprehension, I will do what I like. Conversely, if there is a likelihood of police in the area and, if I offend I will likely be arrested and face charges, I will think twice about committing offences.

At the time of this burglary at least there were officers at Wareham, that could potentially respond, albeit from a distance away. Since then the police cover has been further eroded. From ten pm until seven am there is no police presence at all in the Purbecks. Calls for assistance have to be responded to from Poole, twenty miles away.

Clarke and Hough's 1984 statement was incredibly influential in weakening police management's commitment to patrol, particularly foot patrol. I seemed to hear it continually at management meetings from 1991 onwards, when I was filling in lengthy periods as an Acting Inspector. In response to a 1996 Audit Commission Report, "Streetwise, Effective Police Patrol," my Force set up a working party. All ranks were represented, I was one of the two Sergeants co-opted. The group was chaired by the Assistant Chief Constable, a man who was to have a severe falling out with, whilst an inspector at Headquarters, three years in the future. More on that later.

The working party was a lesson to me on the bureaucratic inertia at the top of most organisations. We discussed police patrol, we visited other forces in an attempt to find the nirvana of best practice. At the end of one meeting the ACC rambled on for ten minutes or so, then left the meeting, I'm sure, very confident that he'd allocated tasks to each of us, to report back on, at the next gathering. As the door closed behind him, we looked at one another, from the highest Chief Superintendent to the lowliest PC, blank incomprehension on all our faces. Then one of us, a Chief Inspector from memory, put us out of our misery. "What is it he wants us to do?" He said, as we all erupted in laughter. A report was later produced, by someone. I can't remember the details. As so often happens in current police culture, none of it made any difference.

The die had been cast by then. The theme of the Audit Commission report was that officers patrolling on foot was impractical in an age when a fast response was expected. The report conceded that the public want to see officers on foot, but it just couldn't happen. Of course, it will never happen if there is no will to do it from the very top.

In the 1980s Weymouth police could count on at least ten officers on parade. By the time of my retirement the average turnout was three. In 1991 My squad would parade ten at Poole Central, another ten split between the two other Poole stations. Those other station were both gone by 2012, only seven officers covering the Poole area. When Mrs Thatcher was Prime Minister, Bournemouth Central would parade twenty officers, with more at the three other Bournemouth stations. By the time David Cameron was at the helm of the nation, two of these stations were gone, Bournemouth Central limping by on four officers. Vast swathes of rural Dorset, that had always been thinly policed, was now empty of officers through the depths of the night, and at many other times of day too.

So where had all these officers gone? Whilst browsing casually through the internet one evening, I came across a PDF of the Dorset Police Annual report of 1977. The time of the Queen's Silver Jubilee, the time when I was an innocent nineteen year old. Once I'd indulged in a trip down memory lane, looking for all the names that I'd first worked with many years ago, my gaze happened on the figures for the year's establishment, or the number of people working for the Dorset Police that year. The number of police officers was reported as 1,092, only 86, or less than 8%, were women. At the time of writing the force has around 1,431 officers, just under 30% of whom are women.

But the figure that caught my eye was the number of non-police officer staff in 1977. The valuable people that worked in administration, finance and personnel, before it became the monster that is HR. This figure stood at 355, 69 of these were cadets or traffic wardens, jobs that no longer exist in the police. So non police staff made up 24% of the workforce, less than 20% if cadets and traffic wardens are excluded. Today, non-police staff total 1,253, or 47% of the total!

Before the 1994 Police and Magistrates Courts Act the number of police officers that any force could employ was set by the Home Office. This was called the force "Establishment." This Act gave chief constables the latitude to employ as many police officers as they wished within their budgets. You may have assumed that chiefs would have gone all out to employ less police staff, as they're now called, and more police, but the above figures do not bear that assumption out. You may also have concluded that the rising number of police staff would free up officers for operational roles, like patrolling the streets. Again, the above figures show this conclusion to be incorrect. So, again, where have all the police officers gone?

Imagine, if you will, a pyramid, long on the base, rising to a pinnacle. This is the police force before 1965, but this model survived in part until the early 1990s. The base of the pyramid is the uniform officers who carry out patrol. They are numerous, carrying out the chores of everyday policing. They are the ones keeping the public safe. Above them are the departments and support arms that feed the base and allow it to carry out its duties. The length of the base reflects the number of officers engaged in the base level of policing, patrolling, deterring crime, acting to protect life and property when required to do so. They are the most numerous of the policing family.

As the 1990s progressed the pyramid slowly began to invert. There are still a few officers carrying out day to day policing, but the priorities of the force have become distorted. The headquarters empires, like training or operations, and new station based departments, have become more important at the corporate level, than those still labouring, doing the real job on the streets.

Those still left at the bottom have become little more than a reservoir, to staff these other departments when they demand it.

To illustrate this, I return to the tragic case of Gaia Pope. As part of their response to criticism levelled at the police during Gaia's inquest, the force declared,"

"Following an independent investigation by the Independent Office for Police Conduct we have delivered many changes to our ways of working and introduced dedicated missing persons teams to ensure our response meets national best practice and provides the right service for our communities."

So, a new team is set up. Some members of those teams may be police staff, some will definitely be police officers. Where will those police officers come from? Probably frontline patrol officers, further denuding their ranks. Surely, it would be more efficient to have had an experienced and highly motivated sergeant on duty the night Gaia went missing, to ensure that the search for her was well directed and properly resourced? This no longer seems to occur to senior police management. If a problem occurs it can only be addressed by setting up new teams dedicated to that problem, irrespective of how it affects the force's ability to staff preventative patrol.

This is a common theme in police risk management. Ian Huntley, a school caretaker, murdered two children, Holly Wells and Jessica Chapman at Soham, Cambridgeshire in August 2002. The government set up the Bichard enquiry, to address the failings in police information sharing, that allowed Huntley to secure the school caretaker job, even though allegations had previously been made against him in respect of assaults on underage girls. This information had not been shared between forces, allowing Huntley to disappear from some radars. In response to Bichard the Dorset Police set up a unit, staffed by police staff members, to ensure the accuracy of data that was processed and shared with other forces. That unit was housed in a large office at Poole Police Station, immediately next to an office I used, immediately prior to my retirement. I noticed that there were always more staff in that office during office hours than there were PCs on patrol in the Bournemouth/Poole conurbation, an urban area with a population in excess of 400,000 people.

In 1998 the force set up a dedicated armed response unit. Forty officers were lost to patrol. An air support unit had been staffed with observers when the force bought its first helicopter in the mid-nineties. More PCs lost to patrol. Information management units were thought to be essential to intelligence led policing, more losses to the frontline. Missing person units, licensing teams, stolen vehicle squads. The story goes on and is repeated. Instead of having regular, systematic patrol, well supervised and resourced with experienced, well trained PCs, there are a small number of very inexperienced officers dashing from call, to call, chasing their tails, until they resign or go sick, always hoping that they can last long enough to get off the streets, and join their fellows, in a squad or unit, that at last gives them some form of status, a status completely lacking these days in the most important and fundamental of police tasks, preventive patrol.

The Bosses

I was promoted to the rank of sergeant in April 1989. I began working as a squad sergeant in the small town of Wareham, an ancient Saxon settlement where the River Frome empties into Poole Harbour. It wasn't my first choice, as if there was any choice in those days, as I had been promised Bournemouth Central. I was young and wanted a busy station. But, that said, I'd made sergeant in less than seven years, and I was feeling pretty pleased with myself.

It was one week day afternoon, about two weeks into my tenure as a sergeant, that I answered a telephone call, informing me that there was going to be major disruption to road traffic between Weymouth and Wareham, the following morning. It appeared that several hundred workers at the Wytch Farm oil field, the largest onshore oil field in Europe, were in dispute with their employers over pay and conditions and, instead of taking the provided buses to work the next morning, as a protest, they were going to walk the twenty miles from the old holiday camp in Osmington, near Weymouth, where they were quartered, along the A352 Road to Wytch Farm. Virtually all that route was the responsibility of the officers of Wareham Station. The potential for severe disruption was obvious.

Thinking that I was on top of all that had to be done, I called the Duty Inspector at Weymouth, on whose patch the march would begin. As fate would have it, he was my old squad inspector. He told me to contact Operations Division at Headquarters, so that an operational order could be drawn up. I dutifully did just that and imparted all I knew to an Acting Inspector, who seemed at something of a loss, but, after a bit of dithering, he told me to leave it with him.

Around half an hour later my office telephone rang again, and, without a care in the world I picked it up.

"Sergeant Hicks." On the other end of the line was a voice that was unmistakable. The Chief Superintendent who was the Western Divisional Commander.

"What the fuck do you think that you're doing over there John?" He spat at me.

"Well Sir, I….."

"Don't fucking talk back to me. I've just had a phone call from some Acting Inspector at Headquarters telling me about some event in my Division. My fucking Division!" My stomach contracted, my self satisfaction at being such a young hot-shot sergeant drained away like water into sand, or like my career down the toilet.

"You never go outside my Division. Do you fucking understand?"

The call went on for what seemed like an hour, but was probably only ten minutes or so. Basically, he was informing me what a fuck up I was. At the end of the call, I could only agree with him.

When I finally and carefully cradled the phone, my thoughts turning to job hunting, his final words, his coup de grace, echoed in my ears.

"John, you've been a sergeant five fucking minutes and I'm going to see to it that you're not a sergeant for even five fucking minutes more!" The buzzing that droned on, as I held the phone to my ear, after he'd crashed his phone down, was like the musical score of a tragic opera.

Over the next week or so I waited for the memo from Divisional Headquarters busting me back to constable. This was a real possibility in those days, as a promotion brought with it a years probation, within which the rank could be lost at the whim of a senior officer. But nothing happened.

A couple of weeks later I had to return to Weymouth to give evidence in some, now, long forgotten court case. I was sitting in the parade room killing time, when the last person I wanted to see in the world appeared in the doorway. The Divisional Commander. Much to my relief, at first, he seemed to remember nothing of his telephone diatribe against me, asking affably how I was, also enquiring about my wife's health, before asking me if I had I seen a particular officer that he was seeking that morning. As he turned to leave a gigantic grin blossomed on his face, as if he was recalling a particularly pleasant memory.

"I gave you a fucking good bollocking a couple of weeks ago, didn't I John?"

"Yes, Sir, you did."

His grin hardened, "Don't worry, I've found out whose fault it was, and given them a fucking good bollocking too." Then he was gone like a whirlwind, leaving me dumfounded, trying to fathom what he meant.

The axiom, "Never apologise, never explain," has been variously attributed to Winston Churchill, Benjamin Disraeli and even John Arbuthnot Fisher, an Admiral of the Victorian era. My irascible boss clearly subscribed to this way of doing business. But he had thrown me a bone. Part of the fault in this matter lay with the Inspector at Weymouth, in that he gave dubious advice to an inexperienced sergeant. He was the other recipient of the bollocking, I was sure. Our little exchange, in the parade room at Weymouth that morning, was as close to an apology as I was ever going to get.

I wouldn't say that this man was typical of the senior officer of the eighties, but his attitude, that I'm the boss, and just do as you're fucking told, was much more prevalent then than it was when I retired. He was a bear of a man, about six feet three and thick set. His father had been a senior officer in the Force, and he'd learned at his father's knee. Even at his exalted rank he wasn't averse to getting out on the streets and arresting miscreants. This was a common occurrence in those days. I've read of well documented stories of Chiefs, like Sir Geoffrey Dear, Chief of the West Midlands Force between 1985 and 1990, and Sir John Stevens, Commissioner of the Metropolitan Police between 2000 and 2005, hitting the streets to gauge the temperature, actually becoming involved in the arrest of violent offenders.

When I was an inspector in the 2005 I was the Community Safety Bronze in an operation that involved a siege at a house where a man was holed up with a sawn-off shotgun. I was responsible for liaison with the local council, and all that entailed. Whilst high on cocaine the man had burst in on his ex-partner and children, threatening to shoot her. When the man fell asleep the woman ran out of the house, dragging her children with her. A four day siege began when the man, now without hostages, refused to give himself up. On day three of the stand-off I received a phone call from the widow of a Chief Superintendent in the Force. Coincidentally, but perhaps not so in such a small Force, she was the widow of the senior officer that had "Told me off" after the incident with Roy in the car park during my probation.

The lady, clearly very angry, told me that the Force was being made to look like total fools. She proudly informed me that, if her husband had been in charge, he would have kicked down the door, ending the siege on day one. After taking into account her natural admiration for her deceased husband, I still have no doubt that this would have been exactly what would have happened in the sixties, seventies and eighties, when strength and manliness would have been more valued qualities than restraint and proportionality. I sympathised with her point of view, but was duty bound to tell her reluctantly that times had changed, and such direct action was only taken these days as a last resort.

The next day the armed man pointed the shot gun at his own chest, ending the stand-off and, unfortunately, his life with it. But I have no doubt that the widow's deceased husband would have been the first through the door if the siege had happened in 1975, not 2005.

Of course not all senior officers of the 1960s, 70s or 80s were paragons of virtue. Eighteen years is a very long time to be a Chief Constable. By the time I joined the Force this particular Chief of my Force had been retired for two years. He was clearly an impressive man in many ways, a Royal Marine officer in World War Two, previously mentioned in dispatches, he'd been wounded in the battle to capture the German Kusten Canal in 1945, during the dying days of the war. Due to service in that action he was awarded the Military Cross. However, during my service I heard multiple stories of how he turned the Force into his personal fiefdom, promoting cronies and using the Force for his own convenience. Although you can't libel dead men, I hesitate to blacken the image of this man, as my intention is not to vilify him, but to illustrate how even the no nonsense senior officers of yesteryear, could allow themselves to behave with less than perfect integrity.

A small example of such behaviour may seem trivial but exemplifies the way that a culture can be corrupted, even if policing itself is being conducted in the best interest of the public. This particular Chief had travelled to a London Airport from which he intended to fly off on a vacation. On arriving at that airport, he discovered that he had left his passport at his home address. A phone call was made, a traffic patrol car was despatched to pick up the passport, speeding up the motorway to deliver the item to the relieved holidaymaker.

It is only fair to point out that the politically correct chiefs of the twenty-first century are not immune to using their position for personal convenience, even as they're scrupulously observing the correct pro-noun etiquette, whilst sedulously promoting equity and diversity. In October 2023 Jo Farrell took over as Chief Constable of Police Scotland, the behemoth brought into being in 2013 by the merger of the eight regional forces North of the border.

Ms Farrell had joined the Cambridgeshire Constabulary in 1991, and by 2019 had risen to the rank of Chief Constable in the Durham Constabulary. After a few days in the job in Scotland Ms Farrell was confident enough, according to a report on the BBC Scotland web site, to declare that Police Scotland was guilty of "institutional discrimination," echoing a statement by her predecessor, Sir Iain Livingstone. Ms Farrell stated that this was a "difficult message" for the Police Scotland staff, but she was determined to drive forward an "anti-discrimination agenda."

Presumably this was the agenda she was pursuing when she ordered a Police Scotland officer to drive her, in a police vehicle, on a 240 mile round trip to her home in Durham, after trains were cancelled due to a storm. Plus ca change, but at least the guys forty years ago knew how to lead when it mattered, and would have had the decency never to have rubbished their own officers and staff in public.

Incidentally, when a Police Scotland Assistant Chief Constable was asked on a Sunday Politics TV programme to give an example of a Force policy that was "institutionally discriminatory" the officer struggled to do so, finally stating that body armour can be ill fitting for female officers. Hardly, a problem that should be used to damn the whole force. I rather suspect that such sweeping statements are for the purpose of ensuring that the right people are aware that those uttering them are onside with the latest agenda item, rather than addressing any real problem that would make the people of Scotland safer. Meanwhile Police Scotland closes police stations, fails to investigate crimes, attends only the most serious incidents and, according to Davis Threadgold, chairman of the Scottish Police Federation, the force is "becoming irrelevant in our communities."

Towards the end of his tenure, in 1978, this Chief who had his passport delivered to the London airport, was asked by Merlyn Rees, the Home Secretary in the Labour government, to investigate allegations of multiple corruption against officers of the City of London and Metropolitan Police, including allegations that the famous Flying Squad were taking bribes from armed robbers for disclosing sensitive information and for "losing" evidence in ongoing investigations. Dorset is a mainly rural Force and you may think that the Home Secretary might have chosen a larger, perhaps more worldly wise outfit, to investigate such serious allegations against, arguably, the most famous police Force in the world. Or perhaps that was the point. This investigation was dubbed "Operation Countryman."

The investigation team soon earned the sobriquet of "The Sweedy," from the officers they were investigating, a pun on the then currently popular seventies TV series, "The Sweeney." The worldly Met officers seemed to have nothing but contempt for the county officers investigating them. Perhaps they had good reason for this attitude. One anecdote related to me by a traffic officer, who had been designated to drive the senior investigating detectives around London during the investigation, amply illustrates this picture.

Two very senior detectives from the Countryman team arrested a Metropolitan Police Detective Chief Inspector one morning for corruption and intended to search his house for evidence. My informant was the designated driver. The DCI told his captors that he didn't have the keys to his house, but his wife was in possession of them at a nearby shop that she owned. On reaching the shop the investigators allowed the DCI to enter and obtain the said keys unaccompanied. In the days before satellite navigation my informant was obliged to rely on the directions of the prisoner to drive to his home address. My informant told me that he had the feeling that he was being directed to the location by a very circuitous route.

When they arrived the said detective's wife answered the door to them before they could insert the key into the lock. The deductive power of Sherlock Holmes is not needed to come to the conclusion that no incriminating evidence was found at the address. In May 1980 the investigation was assigned to another Force. Very few corrupt officers were ever forced to answer for their crimes in court. Senior officers of that era may have been free of the cancer of political correctness infecting current forces, but that does not guarantee that they were competent.

More now on the Assistant, now Deputy, Chief Constable, who had chaired the working group on police patrol. In 1999 I was on top of the world. I was Inspector at Headquarters, in a Department that was a stepping stone to further advancement. I had written a report on the Force adoption of the concept of Problem Oriented Policing, a concept that I really believe in but like most good ideas fall by the wayside of police culture. My Force had trialled POP in a small area, and was looking to adopt the concept Force wide. I interviewed officers that were making use of the concept. I interviewed senior officers that were applying the concept in their divisions. I researched literature that analysed and evaluated applications in the US and in Britain. Growing out of my research was a report that I presented one afternoon to a senior officers group, chaired by the Assistant Chief Constable. My conclusion was that the concept had validity in solving community problems, and making life better for the public, but had been hamstrung, as the ACPO officer who should have been supporting it, had not done so to the required degree. This officer was none other than the current Deputy Chief Constable. The senior officers involved in the pilot had nodded their heads sagely, as I set out my conclusions. They clearly agreed with me.

I had sent the Deputy Chief Constable my report months before, but he had not communicated with me. The morning after my presentation I received an email from the Deputy inviting me to go to his office immediately. I knocked, was admitted, and was told to sit in an area with armchairs as he conversed for an extended period with someone on the telephone, perched behind his desk. After some considerable time, he put the phone down, picking up a document that I saw was a copy of my report. He advanced on me, waving the document menacingly. I'll never forget the words that he spat at me,

"I approach this subject with a degree of personal angst." He exclaimed, thrusting himself down into a chair facing me. He was so animated that I thought for a moment that he might assault me. But instead, he launched into a spittle flecked tirade, rubbishing my report and its conclusions and stating that, "I had only wrote down what people involved told me," which I thought at the time was a rather strange line of defence, and still do. I'd decided that I wasn't going to say anything, I mean there was a gap of five ranks in seniority in his favour, and the police is, or was, a disciplined service. But, as he unfairly demolished months of work, I bridled, beginning to respectfully state my view, that the report was fair and accurate. After a to and fro, of around an hour, he made it clear that the interview was over, his parting comment being,

"I will defend my position vigorously at Chief Officer's Policy Group."

I was never called to participate in such a discussion at COPG. He either scuttled any further discussion in his own interest, or POP became just another fad that came and went, like much else in the police. I left Headquarters to go back to operational policing shortly afterwards. But in the next three years or so I attended two boards for promotion to chief inspector. I was unsuccessful on both occasions. The chair of the board on both occasions? That same Deputy Chief Constable. A year ago I ran into an old colleague of mine, a retired Chief Inspector. He told me that he was on a charity board with the man that I had so upset all those years before, the now retired Deputy Chief. Over a pint I told him the story that I have just related to you. He laughed,

"Come and have a drink when we next meet. I'm sure he's buried the hatchet now." I agreed, I mean what difference does it make now. I still haven't heard from him since that day with the date and location for that drink. I presume the hatchet is not buried in the mind of my old antagonist.

The HBO series "Band of Brothers," chronicles the odyssey of Easy Company, 2nd Battalion, 101st Parachute Infantry Regiment of the US 101st Airborne Division, from the Normandy Landings to victory in Europe, During one episode, as the Company fights off German attacks, in the winter snow during the vicious action in the Battle of the Bulge, the Company is under the command of Lieutenant Dike. The narrator makes the observation that Dike is not a bad leader because he makes bad decisions, he is a bad leader because he makes no decisions.

The most inept senior officers I've worked for were men and women who resembled Lieutenant Dike. If resources were needed for a particular initiative, or a speedy decision on an immediate operational matter was required, these officers would invariably ask for a written business case, that once submitted would often never be heard of again. One night I was Duty Inspector when an illegal rave began in a disused, but dangerous, old industrial building. I had few resources in terms of officers to police it, so I called the Duty Superintendent to request more resources, and to seek his assessment of the situation. He told me that, "Whatever you decide to do John, I will back you." This particular officers was a transferee from another, very large Force, known to be a hotly ambitious, and a keen player in Force politics. In the end I decided that the risk to safety of young people and my officers, of shutting down the rave by force, in an unlit and dilapidated building, was too great. The building was away from residential buildings, and the noise wasn't causing annoyance to the locals. However, had I made the opposite choice, closing the event down by force, and the whole situation turned into a debacle, would that senior officer have backed me if there was any risk to his reputation or prospects? I have my doubts.

The best boss I ever worked with was my Superintendent when I was working as Community Safety Inspector in his Division, in the early years of the century. Community Safety was a concept introduced in the Crime and Disorder Act 1998. It involves the police working in partnership with the local authority, the NHS and other partners to reduce crime and disorder. I was a fan, and luckily for me so was this particular boss. I would telephone him about an idea that I'd had that required money, or human resources, that is officers on the ground. If he liked the idea he said yes on the spot, if he didn't, he let me know. There were no requests for lengthy business cases that took days to complete, only to become lost in some byzantine bureaucracy, or left to collect dust in a neglected in tray.

One morning I called him on some matter or other. He'd been on holiday to the Caribbean, and I asked him if he had enjoyed his break, he snapped back, "Yeah, yeah, get on with it." Rude? Yes, maybe. But I wasn't looking for him to be my mate. I wanted him to give me leadership and decisiveness, which he always did. Police officers pray for a boss like this man, but it appears that nowadays, such senior officers are increasingly rare.

A few years before I retired, another Superintendent asked me to go to Headquarters to a meeting that he didn't fancy. Well, he didn't really ask me. He knew that I'd worked at HQ, and understood the strange arcane language spoken by the inhabitants. The meeting purpose was to discuss the Force's adoption of "activity-based costing." That is the system where every aspect of police work, every activity, can be allocated a cost, and therefore evaluated for its utility. Fine, you may say. But, when we weren't even doing the basics right what's the point? I mean this bullshit can't ever count the cost of having no one patrolling, keeping order in the High Street, when disorder breaks out, when damage is caused, people assaulted.

The meeting was chaired by a Chief Superintendent, who I'd worked for previously and, along with numerous civilian staff from the mighty to the insignificant. There was also another Chief Superintendent who I knew quite well. We'd been promoted to sergeant on the same day. We'd met in the waiting room before standing to attention before the Chief Constable for our ennoblement. I'd also worked for him as an Inspector when he was Operations Chief Inspector in a division. I'll call him Craig.

After the meeting, when my head still spinning from the buzzword bingo, that I'd called silently called "house" to at least three times, Craig approached me, broaching the idea that I should come to Headquarters to work for him. After I respectfully declined his offer, he shook his head, smiled and observed,

"Well, that was a very useful meeting anyway."

As I knew by that juncture, that my aspirations for further promotions were without hope, I felt free to reply,

"Craig, either I'm too thick to understand the airy-fairy concepts that were flying around in there, or everything we've suffered for the last hour is total bollocks." He smiled, a sympathetic smile, a smile that you would bestow on someone who has just suffered banishment to the outer limits. Without another word he turned walked briskly away. I've never spoken to him since.

Now, Craig had been a good practical copper, before he surrendered to Headquarters land. His forte had been public order policing, and he was an authority in that realm. We'd been the two Sergeants on the same PSU during the infamous Leeds United disorder in Bournemouth in May 1990. But he'd clearly recognised that rapid upward progress can be made if you put aspirations to be a real policeman aside, allowing yourself to suffer the sweaty embrace of group speak and sterile managerialism.

Once this truism is recognized, by those that aspire to rapid advancement, that is the path they will take. A particular regime tends to seek to replicate itself in its own image, and this is what happened through the early years of this century. If a candidate speaks the right language, they will stand a good chance of joining the elect. Retired Superintendent Iain Donnelley, in his book, "Tango, Juliet, Foxtrot," that police officers will recognise as representing the phonetic alphabet for, "The Job's Fucked," summed up this problem,

"These people (senior officers) were seemingly divorced from reality and many of them unfortunately believe their own bullshit, which is always dangerous."

This state of affairs seems to have been reinforced in the last few years by the senior police echelons eager embrace of intersectionality. Intersectionality is defined by the Oxford English Dictionary as.

"The interconnected nature of social categorisations such as race, class, and gender, regarded as creating overlapping and interdependent systems of discrimination or disadvantage; a theoretical approach based on such a premise."

This dangerous ideology has elbowed its way to have becoming the dominant ideology in most public services in recent years. It has led to police forces seeming, certainly in the eyes of the general public, to be more concerned about celebrating "Pride Day," or "Black History Month," or policing online "Hate Speech" than preventing burglaries, keeping public order or making sure that citizens do not suffer the adverse effects of anti-social behaviour.

In 2021 a brightly coloured poster bearing the logo of West Yorkshire Police and its LGBTQ Network appeared on the internet. With the aid of drawings of, what appears to be a man with the distended stomach of pregnancy, a turbaned figure with a child and, what appears to be two men, one with his head on the stomach of another, the poster promotes "Trans Parenting Day," 7th November 2021. I have no idea if senior levels of West Yorkshire Police gave permission for their logo to appear on this poster, but a casual search of the internet will reveal that West Yorkshire Police, along with every other force in the UK is fully supportive of the aggressive promotion of the LGBTQ agenda. Police vans bedecked in Pride colours, officers in full uniform with pride garlands around their necks, faces painted in pride colours, are hallmarks of any self-respecting Pride parade.

In 2018 the Chief Constable of West Yorkshire Police, Dee Collins, appeared in a video lauding LGBTQ History Month. She stated that LGBT rights are still being fought for in West Yorkshire, but was not specific about which particular law disadvantaging gay people needs to be fought. She then praised gay activist Peter Tatchell, then, rather strangely, the American drag queen and gay rights activist, Marsha P. Johnson, of whom I'm sure most people living in the dales and cities of West Yorkshire are completely unaware. I had to look her up.

She went on to proclaim,

"Looking at our own Nation's history can show that laws may change overnight social attitudes don't move as quickly."

She then let her audience know that West Yorkshire police officers "have also been asked to understand what makes the lived experience of LGBT different."

"Lived experience" is the type of psychobabble beloved of the new generation of police leaders. Its advantage is, that it rates highly in the lexicon of management speak, while at the same time being so vague as to be meaningless.

But it's the first of Chief Constable Collins assertions that I find most troubling. She seems to be saying that the police should be an agency that promotes social change. In a free society the organ of the state that enforces the law must have no role in the promotion of any changes in social attitudes. Social attitudes are functions of a culture. Any member of that society has the right to promote their view of the type of society that they wish to live in. The first priority of the police is to be impartial. To enforce the law fairly on each citizen, no matter their attitudes to the current social conventions and mores. A person has the right to be treated fairly, even if their views clash with the accepted norms of the ruling class. If, for example, a person is not in favour of same sex marriage, they have a perfect right to hold this view, and express it openly, without any involvement of the police.

The West Yorkshire policing area had the worst violent crime statistics in England and Wales in 2023/2024. 50.8 violent crimes per 1,000 population, the average for England and Wales being 33.4. Perhaps the Force would be better advised to concentrate on the prevention of violent crime in Leeds, on a rainy street at midnight, rather than attempting to shift social attitudes, the first being absolutely their primary task, the latter being not their job at all.

A freedom of information request in February 2025, revealed that West Yorkshire Police employ 19 staff on DEI related matters, at a cost of £1.4 million a year. They also spend a further £361,000 on external DEI training. Just think what that nearly £2 million could do if it was used for frontline policing.

The case of Harry Miller from 2019 is a perfect example of why the police should not act as an agent or as a catalyst for any social change. Mr Miller, an ex- police officer, had posted a series of tweets, in relation to the debate on the reform of the Gender Recognition Act 2004, one of which included,

"I was assigned mammal at birth, but my orientation is fish. Don't mis-species me."

Not very funny perhaps, but did it merit the intervention of PC Gull, a "cohesion officer" from Humberside Police, who contacted Mr Miller by telephone, lecturing him on the fact that he'd hurt some people's feelings. PC Gull also stated, rather portentously that, "I have to check your thinking," even though he admitted that none of the tweets broke the law. It is truly terrifying to me that a police officer could say such a thing, implying PC Gull, and by extension Humberside Police, believe that Mr Miller had committed a "thought crime." The direction for this Stasi like behaviour comes from the very top of policing. The College of Policing, and the National Police Chief's Council. Both have fully embraced intersectionality. This embrace will be catastrophically bad for the law-abiding majority in this country. Those who expect the police to act in the physical environment, not in an Orwellian attempt to control opinions.

Dave Marshall is a recently retired Superintendent who spent a year as lead on national police improvement at the College of Policing. In his recently published book, "The Fall of Policing," he sets out his own views on the reasons why forces find themselves in their present parlous state. He cites, as one of the primary causes of this sorry state of affairs, an obsession with DEI, Diversity, Equity and Inclusion. In other words, intersectionality. This dogma has become entrenched in the promotion process, especially to senior officer level.

"Every interview or promotion board was now crammed full of DEI related questions, replacing the need for the candidate to convey evidence of technical competency."

Any promoter of traditional police skills, like crime prevention or detection, or public safety, were viewed as old fashioned, out of touch with current thinking.

The website of the UK College of Policing proclaims that it supports professional development, sets standards and shares knowledge and good practice. Presumably this body, that costs the taxpayer upwards of £70 million a year, is very influential at the senior level of policing. Unfortunately, Dave Marshall concludes that,

"My main observation of the College of Policing was how little those I engaged with there, understood anything about the realities of policing."

Rather the College seemed to be the "patient zero" of the DEI agenda. Infecting policing with this pernicious agenda, causing the setting up of departments promoting its dogma, consuming money and staff, in forces, where streets are routinely unpatrolled, where people have given up reporting crime.

This is of little surprise when, as Dave Marshall explains,

"Senior Leaders are having their feet held to the fire much more for delivering DEI action plans than they are for improving their operational crime performance."

This leads to many of those senior officers who are,

"Sitting around the mahogany boardroom tables in their crisp white shirts and impressive epaulettes (are senior officers who) have themselves very little in the way of operational exposure."

This cadre of senior officers, those with well developed skills in formulating DEI action plans, but little in the way of operational experience, tends to be self-perpetuating, as they go out of their way to promote others in their own image.

The practice of recruiting non police officers directly to the rank of superintendent is also very worrying. A similar scheme exists for recruiting directly to the rank of inspector. It is inconceivable in my eyes that, a person who has never carried out any duty as a constable or sergeant, could ever adequately appreciate the difficulties or operational challenges faced by men and women in these ranks.

The early signs were not good. In 2019 the College of Policing withdrew an advertisement for the direct entry scheme, and Mike Cunningham, the Head of the College of Policing. issued an abject apology when the advert called for "proven leaders" to apply to the scheme, rather than starting "at the bottom." Rather a strange comment as the service invariably speaks of the frontline constable as the most important part of the team. It appears that this declaration is merely the worst type of cant.

In 2014 the very first direct entry to superintendent, former RAF officer Adam Thomson, caused a great deal of offence, when he published an article in an academic journal, bemoaning the fact that he had to spend 12 weeks on patrol with constables, as part of his induction into the North Yorkshire Police.

"If I was training to be the leader of the council, I wouldn't be asked to do a few mornings with the bin lorry first."

He opined, before declaring sheepishly, when his ill-judged remarks were revealed, to the staff of North Yorkshire Police and the general public, that,

"I have the utmost respect for police personnel at all levels, and any comments I made about how direct entrants are trained were certainly not intended to denigrate the important work that PCs do."

In 2019 the College of Policing paused the direct entry scheme due to a lack of take up from forces. A hopeful sign maybe. But their web site still speaks of the scheme as current, so it hasn't gone away. Maggie Blyth, who had a long career in the Probation Service, before joining Hampshire Constabulary as a direct entry Superintendent in 2016, was appointed as Deputy CEO of the College of Policing in 2023, and is now the interim Chief Constable of Gloucestershire. The subjects of the direct entry scheme are rapidly making their way to the top in a profession where, I believe, they can have little knowledge or sympathy for the constables, sergeants and inspectors who do the real day to day work of policing. This augurs very unfavourably for the future of policing in this country.

The English philosopher and author C S Lewis, in the preface to his 1942 epistolary novel, "The Screwtape Letters," tells us,

"The greatest evil is conceived and ordered (moved, seconded, carried, and minuted) in clean, carpeted, warmed, and well-lighted offices, by quiet men with white collars and cut fingernails and smooth-shaven cheeks who do not need to raise their voices."

Written over eighty years ago, this description, with the addition of some "quiet women," would seem to perfectly fit the senior officer culture of the current police service.

War Stories (Fiction)

He spins the yarn again tonight in the pub, the one about the decayed corpses in the flat. They never seem to get tired of that one. He, black skin, slumped on the yellow and brown patterned linoleum of the kitchen floor. She, naked on the filthy living room carpet, femur, vertical, the rest of her leg gone, eaten by the dog, that they'd petted, taken for walks, loved. It was his last sudden deaths before he retired. He, the Duty Inspector, had been called because it was so bizarre. Putrefaction and dog shit. Always got a good audience for that one. Some of the weaklings walk off, they can't take it. He loves that.

He had a phone call the day after it happened, at home. They were trialing a new programme, the young girl explained. She was calling officers that had been to traumatic incidents, offering support, with her young pretty voice. He laughed. I've never needed any support up to now, he said, all that is part of the bloody job. When he'd put the phone down he felt a bit uncomfortable. He hadn't meant to be rude to the girl. He thought about what she said later that night, as he had a whisky before bed. He was surprised that the bottle, that he'd bought a couple of days before, was almost empty. He mentioned it to his wife. She gave him a look that he didn't understand, but he knew that she thinks he should. He decided that she must have been having a few nips too. He planned to talk to her about that.

He was called in to see the Superintendent about it. To tell him off for his attitude. He'd known Jim Greenoff since they were PCs together, thirty years ago. They both had a good laugh about the whole thing.

"No point in telling you to be more sensitive, you old bastard," Jim had said sipping at his coffee, "See you for a round, next Friday as usual?"

These stories he tells in the pub, or the ones that they all tell when they get together, those old farts who'd got through the thirty years. The meat chopped up by the train, the brains all over the ceiling as they try to dig the bullet out. The young girl, naked on the toilet floor, flesh coming off in your hands as they turn her in the summer heat. All those dead people with stories of their own have sort of become their stories. They say something about them. They say that they were tough enough, strong enough to do what they did for all those years. Half a century ago, when he was first out in the blue uniform, the Job was full of old tough guys. What else was he going to try to be.

The stories he tells no one, are the ones that he thinks about when he reaches for his whisky late at night. The cry of the young boy in the dark stillness, as his mother tells him what his Father has gone. He, in the half light of the garden shed watching the Father, twisting slowly, lifeless eyes studying him, the rope hanging tightly over the beam, creaking in the predawn stillness. He doesn't ever reveal the him that stands staring at the head and shoulders photograph of the girl, perfect and beautiful, the girl that he'd just rolled over on the toilet floor, her flesh peeling away in strips. He's never going to tell those stories.

Blood and Guts

I reached the top of the concrete stairs and moved slowly out on the open top floor of the car park. The level was empty of cars, bathed in orange light. Then I saw them. Both huddled low against the ticket machine, working something long into it, trying to prize it open. There were only two ways down, through me, or down the opposite stair well, the one I'd sent probationer Bill to climb.

I came out into the open shouting at them to stand still. As I expected they skedaddled away towards the opposite stairs, where Bill would be waiting, the jaws of the trap. But instead they disappeared into the black hole of the stairwell, unimpeded, with me in hot pursuit. When I came out into the street, at the foot of the stairs, they'd disappeared. Of Bill there was no sign.

We'd suspected that the car park machine thieves had come from a nearby bail hostel, and soon other officers joined me, responding to my call. It was soon established, by speaking with hostel warden, that two residents had just come in, breathing heavily, perspiring like they'd just run a 400 metre race. They were soon arrested and charged. But that's not the point of this story.

Bill was waiting outside the hostel as we emerged with the thieves. He claimed that he had become lost on the stairs. He reported sick after that. I was an Acting Sergeant at the time. A few days later he came to the station to see me, telling me that he intended to resign. He said that he'd only joined the police because his Father had served. He was certain that it wasn't for him. I wished him well. The Job is not for everyone.

The truth about Bill was that he'd come to our squad from another. It was strongly suspected, a grizzled old Sergeant had told me, that Bill lacked "bottle." I was tasked to put him in situations where that proposition could be tested.

"Bottle," or courage was something much prized during my time in the Job. Bottle shouldn't be confused with brawn. I've worked with big strong mountains of men, I've worked with martial arts experts. But most coppers aren't that. Most are ordinary blokes, not Bruce Lee or Chuck Norris. Bottle is simply the strength of will to have a go. To do your best, to put something on the line in a violent situation. Bill wasn't able to bring himself to do that. No shame. But also, no future in the Job.

Women police officers weren't expected to get stuck on like the blokes, for obvious reasons. But that said, I've never worked with a woman who wasn't willing to give it a go when the chips were down. I worked with one young lady who was a six times world Tae Kwon Do champion. The blokes used to mutter to each other in a macho, half joking way, that they could take her, but I suspect that if they'd tried, she would have laid them out one by one.

The other side of the very macho culture was the ability to witness the most upsetting and gruesome scenes, whilst still functioning efficiently and doing your job. I've seen most things. From gunshot victims, knife wounds, hangings, drownings, when the fish have had their fill of the eyes, nose and the other extremities.

One of the most extreme spectacles is a when a human being comes into contact with a moving train. A man who wanted to commit suicide, but changed his mind at the last moment, the train slicing off his legs as he rolled out of the way. He died in hospital the next day. I won't even begin to describe the man sucked under the wheels of the train as he walked home along the railway culvert whilst drunk. One morning at a small station I was confronted by a pile of grey matter lying on the platform. A man had committed suicide by walking out as a train pulled into the station, head butting the still moving engine. I was Duty Inspector and by the time I arrived the body had already been moved, but for some reason the poor souls brain matter was still in situ. One bonus for local police from railway deaths, the matter will ultimately be dealt with by British Transport Police, who have jurisdiction on railway property.

Back in the early 2000s a man that I had been a PC with in the 80s was promoted to DI. His first suspicious death must have set him up for the rest of his career. Out in the sticks a walker had made a horrific discovery, a headless body sat in the driving seat of a car in an isolated car park. The first theories were based on the idea of a gangland killing, an exhibition to send a message, to encourager les autres. It was only when a rope tied to a gatepost was found nearby, followed by the missing head being discovered in undergrowth, that the strange truth dawned on the investigators. DNA found on the rope confirmed that the, clearly,very disturbed man, had tied the rope around his own neck, before driving off at speed, thus severing his head from his body. The mental state that this poor soul must have been in, to fashion such an inventive end, can only be guessed at.

My last sudden death was one of the most bizarre. I was Duty Inspector. I was at a police station speaking to the Sergeant. A call came in that a PC had been called to a first floor flat, where two bodies had been discovered. The PC had called supervision as the scene that he'd come upon was quite unusual. As Duty Inspector I went with the Sergeant to the scene.

The flat was up a flight of stairs from the road. At the top of the stairs was a kitchen. Sat of the floor was a deceased male who had clearly been there for some time as his skin had turned black. The flat smelled strongly of faeces. To the right was a living room where a naked female corpse lay. She was on her back with one of her legs extended into the air. From the knee down this leg no longer existed. The tibia and fibula bone and flesh were gone, some of the femur was also missing.

The PC told me that a dog had run off as he opened the door to the flat. It appeared that the dog had subsisted by eating its owners.

I am proud to say that every one of my colleagues over my thirty-year career carried out their duties in respect of these horrendously distressing incidents with the upmost professionalism. They may have had to take a moment to process their feelings, or to find a secluded spot to throw up, but they did that after they'd carried out to the letter what they were required to do.

For me, it wasn't the gore that sometimes got to me. It was the all too human aspects of incidents, the small nuances that revealed that the corpses, the bodies that were the property of the coroner, had loved ones, had stories that had ended. A hanged man in the depths of the night. His wife who'd discovered him. The cry of his twelve year old son, in the mist and darkness, as she told him what had happened to his Dad. Me, in the garden listening. Or the one year old, dead in his cot the morning after a wedding party. His trouser suit hung on the bedroom door, worn so proudly the night before. A life that would never be. These are the type of events that haunt you.

Wind Ups

Staff in the NHS have come under some quite scathing criticisms from some quarters, about the seemingly endless, dancing, singing and formation trolly ballet, that appeared on the video sharing app TikTok during the time of Covid. Perhaps people feel let down that, whilst they were outside on Thursday evenings banging their pots and pans, local hospital staff were spending their time devising elaborate routines that wouldn't have shamed Busby Berkeley. I haven't a problem with the videos because, I'm absolutely certain that should a patient have needed attention, the TikTok would have been cast aside, and the stethoscope and the bed pan taken up in good time.

When I was promoted to the rank of Inspector in October 1998, I was posted to our Force Headquarters, onto a department grandly named, "Quality and Development." This was a department that was supposed to drive change and innovation in the Force. I was posted there as, it was the opinion of senior officers, that I was proficient in getting ideas down in writing. Many readers of this book may now be debating the wisdom of this opinion, but, be that as it may, I was there, proudly, with my two new shiny pips on each shoulder on the first Monday in my new job. The department's mantra was "continuous improvement," bear in mind this was in the early years of the Blair era, when no version of change was bad, and there seemed to be limitless pots of money to enable some of the worst ideas in human history, such as the Private Finance Initiatives, to gain flight. PFIs are arrangements when a private company enters into a contract with a police force, or a hospital trust, or any public body to build and operate a facility in exchange for, in some cases, land, in almost all cases, a contract to run that facility for twenty-five or thirty years. True, the building is delivered, sometimes, sometimes not, see the Royal Liverpool Hospital disaster, but the service costs exacted by these contracts were, and are, ruinously expensive. I have heard of instances where, the moving of a photograph to a new location, cost the force over a hundred pounds.

Many of the staff in the Quality and Development Department were civilian staff. Recruited for their own skills, skills that police officers could not provide. One was an older man, that I worked quite closely with on a number of projects. He'd been a "Time and Motion" man in industry before he'd thrown his lot in with the police. He'd patrolled various industrial concerns with his stopwatch, breaking down production into segments that could be timed and valued and made to be more efficient by judicious tweaking. He was a lovely affable man, but he had an annoying trait. He believed that police work was the same as an assembly line. As long as there was someone on each station of that line it didn't matter who that was. He championed a concept called "annualised hours," that held that a worker had only a responsibility to work a set of promised hours, and when these hours were worked, and who he/she worked with, was immaterial.

I tried to explain to him that, if your objective was to make sausages, then any person, standing or sitting, at any stage of the process could carry out their limited activity that went to the making of the good old banger, that would rest appealingly on someone's breakfast plate. When the hooter went, when they went home to their families, the job would be exactly the same the next morning, when the machine started again, and the sausage meat began to flow. This is even true of a much more skilled profession, such as nursing. Before I feel the wrath of my caring profession readers, or my own son who works in the NHS, I'm not saying that nurses are less skilled than police officers, far from it. I am stating quite categorically that the jobs are of a different nature. Let me explain.

When a nurse goes home after a shift, another nurse takes over the care of the patients that he/she had been caring for on that shift. When that nurse comes back to work the following day those patients may still be there, with the same or slightly different needs. Or there may be different patients, with other needs, who have been looked after by other nurses during the night. The point I'm trying to make is that if a different nurse came on duty every shift change, who were all equally skilled, it would make no difference to patient care. Police work is not like that.

Police work demands a certain continuity. This is partly because police work is spatial as well as incident driven. Officers cover a certain area. This is particularly true of Home Beat Officers or Teams. They cover an area, and the problems of that area are owned by them, or should be. If an officer arrests an offender, or deals with them by way of interview, and that person is charged, that officer is responsible for compiling a file of evidence that will be passed to the Crown Prosecution Service, forming the basis of the material used in that offender's prosecution in court. So, when an officer finishes a shift, the work picked up on that shift will usually not end there. The crimes that he has picked up to investigate will be an issue that must be addressed over several shifts. The prosecution file of the offender charged and bailed the day before will have to be completed within a timed period.

But another objection to my colleagues championing of annualised hours, and an objection that is equally as important as the need to provide the problem solving and administration continuity, is the efficiencies produced whilst working in teams. I'm very lucky, I've always worked in teams where the team ethos was good. We were friends as well as colleagues. We would go the extra mile for each other, appreciating that each individual's safety rested in the hands of all.

This is not always the state of affairs that pertains. In the 1990s I was a Sergeant in a busy station in a medium size town. My team had worked an early shift and had handed on the car keys to the late shift who were parading for duty, while my men and women caught up with paperwork, or were dealing with prisoners in the cells. The shift that we'd handed over to was known to be an underperforming bunch, whose Sergeants were jaded and lacking in motivation. Suddenly, as my guys munched on a sandwich, or signed off a statement of evidence, the radio channel erupted into life with the calls of an officer for assistance, and the appeals from the control room for officers to respond. To our absolute disgust, but not surprise, the late shift sat still, listening the registration numbers of stolen vehicle, or wanted persons, read out in the bored monotone of their Sergeants. Not one of them rose, snatching up the keys, running to their vehicles to assist a fellow officer in danger. I still remember the pride I felt when my officers ran into the parade room, scooped up the car keys from the desk, heading out at top speed to respond to the call for assistance. What particularly sticks in my mind was that the officer calling for help was a member of the team that sat inactive, whilst he faced danger. They had no team ethos. So what has this got to do with NHS staff and elaborate TikTok videos? Well, perhaps these videos were their way of creating something unique to their team? A way of making themselves part of something special, something that bonded them together when the country was seemingly facing an unprecedented threat? Up until the late nineties the police had their own means of doing this. The medium was different, not so public and high tech, but there was a considerable amount of ingenuity shown in each instance.

In the nineties I wrote several pieces for the Police Review Magazine. The Police Review had been first published in 1893 as the Police Review and Parade Gossip. It was a weekly magazine that almost everybody at least flicked through at the time of my joining the police in 1982. It was an entertaining read, featuring the contributions of both serving police officers and influential criminologists, and it was informative too, with a weekly section on sample questions from the promotion exams, as well as exercises on the three areas that the exams tested, criminal law, traffic law and general police duties. At the time Police Review was under the editorship of an ex-cop, Brian Hilliard, who rose to the rank of Inspector in the Metropolitan Police, seeing service in the controversial Special Patrol Group, before becoming a journalist. Unfortunately, the magazine was later taken over by Janes Information group, becoming less a magazine about policing, and more of a magazine for police managers. The magazine was further acquired by American company IHS in 2007 and ceased publication in November 2011.

In the mid-nineties Police Review published an article penned by me, entitled "Learning to Laugh." In it I wrote about the universal police practice of "winding up" the new probationer constable. The habit of playing practical jokes on the newest constables, those that were least likely to believe that they were being set up. Those most likely to doubt that their supervisors and the control room would conspire against them. I was at that time in favour of such practical jokes, they seemed to me to be a harmless way of initiating the young constable into the life of the shift.

When this article was published I was performing an aide to CID, a short term, usually six month attachment to CID for career development. I was a Sergeant at the time and such attachments for sergeants were unusual. I was contacted by the Head of CID, a Detective Chief Superintendent, who told me that the BBC had requested that the force allow me to be interviewed on the article by BBC radio. The Chief Superintendent told me that although it was my decision, as to whether I was interviewed or not, the Chief Constable had let it be known that he was not in favour of such an interview. At that time I had ambitions for promotion to inspector. I therefore considered it circumspect to decline the BBC's kind offer. There is no doubt that both the Detective Chief Superintendent and the Chief Constable had been the subject of, and players, in such "wind ups," in their more junior days, but the winds of change were blowing through the nineties, and practical jokes, involving supervisors and control room, were to become relics of a fondly remembered, but unrecoverable past.

In the era of protecting everyone from hurt feelings, ushered in by a new century, any supervisor playing a practical joke on a constable that resulted in the victim complaining to more senior management, would face discipline proceedings and probable dismissal. "Wind ups" disappeared into the dustbin of history. But here, just for you, I'll relate some of those that I have knowledge of. I'm not saying I was involved of course. I'll take the fifth amendment on that, refusing to incriminate myself.

My own story involves a dog and the control room. One dark winters night in early 1983. It was around four in the morning. I was on foot patrol in the town centre. There was nothing happening. So, just like the makers of TikToks, four decades later, no meaningful work was being impinged upon. I received word from the control room that an owner of a valuable dog, an Australian breed, had got loose in the town centre, and I should keep an eye out for it. Sure enough, I walked around a dark corner in a side street and there was a dog, standing obligingly still, tail wagging, in the middle of the road.

I sidled up to it, holding out my hand as if it contained some tasty treat. The dog, who was a funny little chap, the head of a Chihuahua, the body of a Staffy, seemed pleased to see me. It's a measure of how it easy it was in those days to fool probationers that I didn't question the credentials of such an unprepossessing mutt. It helped that I love dogs, preferring them to people in many cases. Digger, as that was the name that the control room told me was his, allowed me to pick him up, carrying him, as instructed by that control room, to the sea front, where it was said that I would be met by the Sergeant.

Little did I know that the other members of my team had secreted themselves in dark alleys and shop doorway, watching the antics with glee. On reaching the sea front the control room called me up, no doubt primed by the observers on the ground that Digger was now in my arms, and informed me, "463, on no account pick the animal up. It will damage it and render it worthless." As you can imagine, by the time the Sergeant arrived a few minutes later, the dog was standing firmly on the wet ground. We drove back to the station and "Digger" was placed back in the pen in the yard. Once again the poor stray that he was. I never saw Digger again, but I hope he found a good life wherever he ended up. From that time on I was always "Digger" to my colleagues who were on duty with me that night.

"Wind ups" used to take many forms. There were scenarios where dummies were extensively used. All of these set ups were ones that I can personally vouch for as authentic. A heavy dummy, borrowed from the fire brigade, placed across the road in a dark location. The new probationer is out with the Sergeant. The Sergeant drives over the dummy, gets out, goes back, examines the dummy, backs off as if in horror. The probationer wants to know what's happened. The Sergeant orders him to keep his mouth shut. They return to the station where the Inspector calls the team in, informing them that the Sergeant's car has been involved in a fatal RTA, and that the logbook hasn't been filled in. Who was the driver? The Sergeant looks across at the probationer, shaking his head to keep schtum. The probationer can no longer stand it, bolting from the room, pursued by the Sergeant. Before he can be shepherded back in, the dummy has been retrieved and placed in the seat where the probationer had latterly been sitting. The probationer, on returning to the room, looks at the Sergeant on catching sight of the dummy and exclaims, "You fucking bastard Sarge!" Everyone laughs, slapping the probationer on the back. Everyone then recalls their own personal wind up.

I know that this story is true, because I was that Sergeant. When that probationer has completed his probationary period, he was moved to the other end of the county. I didn't meet him again for around fifteen years. I ran into him during a demonstration in London, organised by the Police Federation, against the austerity policies of the first Cameron government. After a greeting, the first thing he mentioned was that incident in the dark with the dummy, over a decade and a half before. It's something that you don't forget.

Dummies are very versatile aids to the nocturnal wind up. A dummy placed on a small island in a lake, allied to the judicious placing of seemingly discarded clothing at the lakeside, after a circulation on parade that a person has gone missing, wearing that exact get up. An officer seeing a body, twenty yards from shore, hesitating, then being told by the Acting Inspector by radio to get in if the person may still be alive. The victim carrying the dummy overhead, back to the shore, illuminated by the headlamps of several police cars, to the applause of his colleagues, his boots full of duck shit. Again, I was that Acting Inspector. A dummy thrown off a tall building in the view of the victim, to land where another officer is waiting to jump up and run off, to the shock and consternation of the victim as he approaches. Sure that he had a dead one. I wasn't involved in that one.

Mortuaries are also fertile ground for wind ups. Hospital staff in those days were more than willing to cooperate in a little harmless fun. The probationer told to examine a body in cold storage for any signs of trauma. The drawer is opened, and the body rolled out. It is traumatic for anyone to examine a dead body for the first time. As the nervous probbie stoops, to remove the white sheet from the body, the corpse, of course another joker, jumps up with a spine-chilling shriek and the poor subject of the joke flees in terror.

Another variation on this theme, and perhaps a joke that could be played on the same subject, is telling him that he would be the person pretending to be the corpse. He would be placed in cold storage, being left to stew for a while in the frigid dark. He would then start to hear a low moaning coming from an area close to him. Of course, another joker had been placed in a nearby storage unit and was the source of the moaning. The discomfiture of the subject is amplified, as he has no way of exiting cold storage until his colleagues liberate him.

It is possible to execute a wind up without any physical action at all. In the early nineties I worked on squad that contained a young officer who used to drive his Fathers's Ford Sierra to work. It was his pride and joy. One night that young man was despatched to a bogus job with another chaperoning officer, a long way from the equally bogus scene that was the subject of the wind up. The job was something like, suspicious persons seen at such and such a location. When the subject was well out of the way, an officer radioed in that he was following a suspicious vehicle, giving the registration number for a Police National Computer check. Of course, the number given related to the vehicle proudly driven to work by the subject of the joke. There then followed a harrowing follow, when the ghost vehicle refuses to stop for police, crashing into various items of road furniture, ending up careering into a wall, before bursting into flames, a story related in the radio transmissions of several chasing officers. Of course, the real vehicle had never left the police yard. The whole scenario had played out on UHF airwaves, and also in the fevered mind of the unfortunate subject of the jape.

In the years that I was involved in these escapades, no one complained or felt humiliated by them. Of course, it could be said in the climate of the time that no one would complain, even if they did feel some frisson of humiliation or bullying. That could be true but, in my belief, wind ups or practical jokes, had a positive effect on the esprit de corps. Perhaps, when the social pendulum swings to another angle, when people are less sensitive to the slightest feeling of offence, wind ups will return.

Mug Shots (Fiction)

The old police station was broken down and surplus to all requirements. It was late at night. He was on the third floor, not used for years. The same corridor where he'd begun thirty years before. The parade and locker room had been there. Now just dust and debris. The old sergeant's office had been used as a junk room for years. In two weeks they would all be gone. Everything would be gone.

An hour before he'd been in the cells, doing reviews. Speaking to the prisoners still awake. Telling them why they had to stay in custody. Writing the same old stuff on the same old sheets. At the new nick it would all be electronic. Typing all that stuff on. All of it being stored in some place that he couldn't even imagine.

One kid had been kicking off, booting the cell door, screaming shit at all, at everyone. By the time he'd got around to speaking to him the kid was crying. He opened the cell flap, the lad was sat on the bed, big fat tears rolling down his face, shoulders slumped, beaten dog, defeated. He'd told the Gaoler to let him in and he'd sat next to the boy. How many of these tough guys had he seen over the years?

"You've got to stay here tonight son, so that we can talk to you in the morning about the burglary that we think you did." The boy was wailing. For no reason that he could explain to himself, he put his arm around his trembling back. The look of disgust on the Gaoler's face, the Sergeant was there too. They think I've gone mad. Perhaps I have. When the kid put his head on his shoulder it drove them away.

After a while the boy stopped sobbing and was calm. He wondered how this little boy had ever ended up in this terrible place. He wondered why he still wondered. After all these years of none of this making any sense to him. He left the kid lying down on his bed, making little sobbing noises. He watched him through the hatch as the sobbing subsided, replaced by little wet snores.

He wrote up the sheets. The Sergeant and the Gaoler ignored him as if he wasn't there. The Sergeant buzzed him out of the block. He heard him whisper "wanker" as the door clunked shut. Years ago he would have gone back in, had him up the against the wall by his shirtfront, but you couldn't do that anymore. It didn't seem to matter enough to him now anyway.

He checked the computer. Nothing much happening. The normal shit. It would be his last night here. He decided that he would go up to the third floor where he'd begun. His first Sergeant, who had got drunk at a party and threw his wife over a hedge. His tutor, who had split up with his wife while he was tutoring him, crashing the car into a wall when he fell asleep at the wheel. When he used to go home on meal break on nights, to the police flat behind the nick, to cuddle his new wife, until the Sergeant told him that was a bad idea. He'd winked at him, obviously thinking that they did other things other than cuddle. He stopped on the first landing. He looked out at the twinkling lights of the town and wondered where his wife was now. The Job is killing you she said.

The old sergeant's office was all dust and litter and fag burns on the blackened desk. His first Station Sergeant was on Gloucester Hill, in Korea, in April 1951, two and half years as a prisoner of the Chinese. If a young constable went into his office without permission, he would be met with a loud "Fuck off, until I invite you in." But if you had a real problem, there was no greater friend. He had a dog that he would never tire of talking about. He presumed that he, and certainly the dog, were long dead.

On the table was a blue, plastic covered folder. It stirred memories in him. It was covered in a thick film of dust, and smelled of nicotine and indifference. It was two foot square and heavy, as if it knew of its own importance. He knew what it was. Before the advent of computer-generated photographs, crime victims would be asked to view these folders, to pick out, perhaps, the persons that had wronged them. Page after page of small black and white photographs of all sort of criminals, twelve on each page, frontal and in profile, He sat on a chair that creaked in protest. A chair that had once done good service, but could be relied upon no more. He looked through all the pages taking time to look into each cold white face. A board, displayed in front of every miscreant, gave his name, date of birth, and the date the photo was taken. All were taken between 1976 and 1980. He recognised many faces, some he could name without the benefit of the board. There were thieves, burglars, those charged with criminal damage or assault. All male. He was surprised at how few were drug dealers, or robbers. Most had long and unkempt greasy hair, he could almost smell their shiny clothes, their tobacco breath.

One of the strip lights in the ceiling flickered for a few seconds, then went out. He sat there for a long time staring at the photos. He remembered how most of them had been pleasant and compliant as he dealt with them. As he took their photo, inked their hands for the four sets of prints. There was no bitterness, no animosity, it was almost as if they were reluctant participants in a game, a game in which they had no choice but to play, but one that they knew they would always lose.

He knew many by name, many others by their faces. He closed his eyes, walking through the years, the memories, the feelings. He wanted to experience some nostalgia, some affection, for a time when he was young and the world stretched before him, ripe with possibilities, but all he could muster was a dreadful miasma of waste, of pointlessness and loss. More than half of his life he'd given it, and his family. Yes, his family, what had happened there? He still had no clear idea.

His watch said four o' clock, 0400hrs. The lowest ebb. The time when all you want to do is sleep. Your body is asking you, what are you doing awake now, if you had any brains at all you'd have a decent job, with regular hours. He dozed, caught himself, the photo album slipping from his fingers, hitting the floor with a deep thud that woke him. As he picked it up a photo became dislodged from its mount, slipping again to the floor. He picked it up, glancing at it, then tossed the album onto the desk, bringing the single photo near to his face.

Yes, I remember him. The photo had yellowed with age, but the face and profile were clear. He was wearing a leather jacket, his shiny hair gathered on top of his head, as if someone had just dragged him along by it. On his cheek there was an open wound, black, like it he had a second mouth. He was laughing in both photos, as if he had just played the best practical joke ever on the entire world.

That night he hadn't thought about for a long time. He was bigger and tougher than him, he was sure. I'm going to kill myself he'd said, walking off from him. He could see the street. He could see the black of the road that he'd dragged him down onto. He could feel the shocks as he fell on him. The unbelief on his face as this scrawny little copper pinned him down, kept on him, until other hands had dragged him up and taken him in. The feeling of the wet road draining through his trousers, the taste of blood in his mouth. The wonder at what he'd done. The smiles of his squad, the new found respect. He'd built a career on it, but it was a sham, false, he taken him down from behind. He was no fighter, he was a fraud. Six months later the man had killed himself anyway. Taunted by his girlfriend, he doused himself in petrol. He was thankful he didn't go to that. His guard slipping, he'd said that he was sorry that it had happened. He'd been laughed at by everyone.

"One less shit to worry about."

After a year or two he agreed. That was the only way to be. Walk on the corpses of dead babies whilst not losing any sleep. Don't even think about it for a second.

A thin light had begun to drain in through the paint peeling iron windows. In a couple of hours he'd hand over, be free of it all for a while. He became aware that he was grinding his teeth. Still two hours. The darkness seeped away. A great emptiness, like an endless void poured over him, filling him with nothingness.

He went back to the cells, banged on the door, saw the look, between the Gaoler and the Sergeant, through the hatch.

"No reviews Sir. All done." The Sergeant stepped back as he snatched the keys from the hook on his belt. The cell door creaked as it swung to. The boy jumped up, his eyes unseeing, sleeping awake. He knelt down before him, the boy's eyes flicked open, he flinched back as if he was deflecting a punch. He grabbed the boy to each side of his body.

"Get out of this fucking life son," he said, and he said it again, and again and again, as the cell light went out, and a feeble dawn light poured in through the tempered glass of the cell window.

Crooks

Until 2013 the Police Staff College was housed in the Italian Renaissance glory of Bramshill House, nestling in the gentle greenery of the Hampshire countryside. The house was first built in the early seventeenth century by the 11th Earl of Zouche, a favourite of King James Stuart, the 1st of England, and the 6th of Scotland. The house was acquired by Sir John Cope in 1699, remaining in the Cope family until 1935. In 1953, by now a grade 1 listed building, it came into the possession of the British Government, becoming the National Police College in 1960. The College housed the National Police Library.

Over two decades ago I happened to be scanning the shelves in that library, when my eyes fell on a pamphlet, "Recidivism: Towards a Solution," written by an ex-offender who had taken the nom de plume, Anthony Crook. He described most criminals as a "rag bag of useless individuals," who are, "people whose aspirations far outweigh their abilities, and they are forever seeking a short cut to leisure at someone else's expense."

As the contemplation and appreciation of beauty in the modern era has been overtaken by the politics of the balance sheet and the bean counter, this beautiful building has been sold off. The magnificent library relocated, to some sterile soulless environment, under brutalist steel and glass. But Mr Crook's description, of the motivation of the typical criminal, is still as relevant today as it was when I sat at that age stained-table, in the baroque splendour of Bramshill.

In the 1993 film, "A Bronx Tale," Robert De Niro plays Lorenzo Anello, a working man, who is trying to prevent his young son, Calogero, from falling under the spell of the local wise guys. Lorenzo tells Calogero, "It don't take much strength to pull a trigger, but try to get up every morning, day after day and work for a living. Let him try that and we'll see who's the real tough guy." That's what my Father did. Got up and went to work every working day, for fifty-six years, keeping my Mother and me.

Although not a Mafioso Don, the average criminal is incapable of such self-discipline and hard work. They want the rewards that work can bring, but the work side of the equation is anathema to them. When I was a custody officer, the sergeant responsible for the processing and welfare of those in police custody, and later as an inspector reviewing prisoners in the cells, I would see the same old lags, years in prison, who were useless at any task they set themselves, be it breaking into cars, or sheds, or people's houses. They would prevail for a while and then be caught. The pathetically weak criminal justice system would impose a very short custodial sentence, that would serve as a rest for them, or a fine, that they wouldn't pay, or a community penalty, like community service, that they wouldn't complete, with no penalty at all for their non-compliance. True, some young tearaways grow out of prolific offending, as they pass into their thirties or forties and take on, however tentatively, the responsibilities of a wife and family. However, a great number do not, continuing their haphazard and incompetent life of crime, until drink, or drugs, or old age, render their broken bodies incapable of the physical act of offending.

But there are classes of criminals that are proficient at what they do. I'll break these down into three categories, there are many more such categories, but these I have chosen will amply illustrate the type of person who will choose to live a life of crime, and be relatively successful, at least in the short term.

The first of these are those that practice serious acquisitive crime. Burglary, robbery, or theft. In the nineties I had dealings with a man, about my own age, who made a serious living from these activities. He lived on a council estate, the head of a gang of his confederates, who I had first dealings with carrying out ram raids on cash and carry premises, particularly during the Christmas season. They were very successful at this, their vehicle of choice being the powerful Jeep Cherokee, always stolen of course. The flimsy walls of the prefabricated warehouse buildings were no match for their attack. Tobacco and alcohol, particularly spirits, were their targets. It is a sad fact that there are a great many people, who are otherwise law abiding, who are willing to dishonestly receive such goods, if the price is right.

When concrete bollards mushroomed impeding and preventing such raids, he and his gang graduated to a more sophisticated variety of larceny. They recruited a man that installed burglar alarms, and was willing to feather his nest outside the law. They specialised in raiding sub post offices at night. Their boffin would neutralise the alarm, the gang disappearing into the dark with ten of thousands of pounds in cash. At one time in the mid-nineties, the gang was the number one target for the Regional Crime Squad. They were eventually nicked, of course. At great cost, both in finance and manpower. They were tracked over a long period of time, being caught in the act inside a remote village post office. Time in jail.

When he came out security had improved. Consumer durables had been made cheap by mass production with low-cost labour in China. TVs and DVD players were not worth the risk of stealing. But there was another avenue outside the law, where money could be made. Drug dealing, no complainants, just customers. An activity with very low risk. I understand that this man moved on and became a player in that field. I still encounter him sometimes in Tesco. Our eyes meet, but we don't acknowledge each other.

Violence is something that most people have little experience of. Children have fights. There may be the odd dust up at school. Football or rugby matches may see some punches thrown. A young man may pick up a bloody nose in the street at closing time. But, in Britain, in the modern era, violence is something that people see in films, or witness in news reports from far away war zones. But there are a cohort of men, and nearly always men, few in number, that live by violence. It's what they do. I met only a few of them, but I'll tell you about one.

I first met him, I'll call him Tom, when I was a Sergeant at a small station in the Purbeck Hills. After a road rage incident he'd exploded from his car, punching a jagged dent in the bonnet of a young couple's car. He was arrested several days later and brought to the station. The Tom I saw was quite small, no more than five feet seven, but muscled and rounded. He was very compliant, charged with criminal damage and bailed to court.

A year or so later I was moved to an urban station covering the estate where this man lived. I began to hear stories of Tom's fighting prowess. Whilst working as a doorman, he'd laid out twelve men, one after another. He'd borrowed the car of another local hard man, dented the wing, posting the keys back through the hard man's letter box without explanation. The hard man had let it be known that Tom would pay for what he'd done. On hearing these threats Tom had confronted the source. The incident concluded with the hard man in tears, kneeling, and kissing Tom's feet. It was said that he'd seen service in the French Foreign Legion, even that he was writing a book about his experiences.

My next encounter with Tom was one bank holiday weekend. I was out one evening with a van crew made up of Special Constables, usually very well meaning, civic minded people. Fine for policing carnivals, but hardly the best complement for a public order incident. Control room directed us to a pub where it was said that Tom had turned over the pool table whilst threatening bar staff.

On arrival, not wanting to inflame the situation, I directed the specials to remain in the van, whilst I went into the bar to see what was happening. Tom was there, along with his wife. He approached me, his face was inflamed, he was blown up, his arms thrust out from his sides. I took a step back, my hand on the handle of my baton.

"You and me. In the toilets. You can use your stick."

"Just calm down mate," I said, "You're in enough trouble already." I knew that I was the one in trouble, maybe heading for a hiding.

Suddenly from nowhere a curly, dark-haired man thrust himself between us. I recognised him as a Traveller, who I'll call Jobie, a man well known to police, as he'd been shot at least three times, during beefs with other Travellers.

"I'll get him home Sergeant. Leave it to me." Tom seemed to calm down. He sat down in the corner of the bar with his wife, who was crying, little sobs, a paper hanky to her eyes. The bar staff didn't want to make any complaint about the incident. A taxi was called. I retreated outside, telling the van load of Specials to go around the corner out of sight. I waited, alone in the car park, to make sure Tom left.

After a few minutes he emerged. After looking around, fixing his gaze on me, he strode purposely, giant steps, in my direction. I could see that he was hyperventilating, again, his massive arms were pumped out from his sides. I withdrew my Arnold baton, a yard long nylon stick that we used at the time, from its carrying ring at my waist, holding it concealed behind my back. I turned sideways. I remember thinking that I might get one blow in before the inevitable conclusion of the upcoming, but unequal, scrap.

He halted a yard away from me and seem to deflate like an indecisive balloon.

"Sorry about that in there," he declared, his voice high, almost feminine.

"It's women they wind you up sometimes, don't they?"

The taxi arrived. Jobie, Tom and his wife entered and purred away to who knows where, leaving a very relieved Sergeant standing in the car park.

A short time later Tom went to the house of a woman with whom he was having an affair. He was under the impression that she was unfaithful to him. She was so terrified of him that she ran out of the house, seeking refuge in the house of a nearby friend. She called the police, a PC was sent and I attended too. When I arrived the woman was in conversation with Tom on the landline, this being a time before the widespread use of mobiles. I could hear him threatening her life, as well as threatening to subject her to all sorts of sexual indignities. I took the handset from her, telling Tom to come outside, as he was going to be arrested.

By this time a crew of police had attended the scene along with a dog unit. Tom came out of the house. I arrested him for making threats to kill. He offered no resistance. I sat in the back of the police car on the way to the station and, just before we drove through the gates, Tom turned to me and said,

"You know what I could do to you if I wanted don't you?"

"Calm down Tom. I have no illusions at all about that."

He smiled at me and said, "Well, don't harbour any." It was at this point that I understood that this was a very dangerous, unstable, madman, that was capable of anything.

After he was booked into custody and placed in a cell the duty DS came into the cell block, telling us that, before Tom had called the woman, he had raped her fourteen year old daughter. After he was charged and remanded in custody, a number of women came forward to allege that Tom had been beating up their husbands for a long time, then he had repeatedly raped them. In my service I came across very few men as dangerous as Tom. But they do exist.

Fraud. That's what people do to banks, or insurance companies, isn't it? But there is another type of fraud, in my experience a largely hidden problem, because the victims either don't know that they've been victimised, or, are too embarrassed to admit that they were. I'm speaking about the disgusting deviants that prey on old people.

1996 saw me working in CID in a busy urban station. I was a uniform Sergeant, but was temporarily attached to the CID to gain experience. An elderly man had complained that a jobbing builder had driven him to a cash point, making him withdraw money to pay for work on his house. Work that had not been done. The crooked builder had told the old man that he would return for more money, and a panic alarm had been fitted, so that the victim could activate it when his tormentor returned, so alerting officers. This occurred and the builder had been arrested. I was allocated to deal with him. This man was very talkative, soon amazing me with incredible stories of the sub class of criminals that made their living from conning vulnerable elderly people. One woman, who I will call Ada, was prominent in many of these stories. I began to actively pursue Ada's activities, activities that were perpetrated on, for the most part, on vulnerable victims.

Ada had been married to a man who operated in the building trade, being well known for quoting high and delivering low, or not at all. This was in respect of mainly elderly customers. Even though they had been separated for some time, he still shared the knowledge of his victims with Ada. She would visit them, some months after their unfortunate contact with her husband, and inform them that they had not paid VAT on the work done. It was a source of amazement to me that most victims would not query this, parting with large sums of money that bore little relation to the current rate of VAT.

I learned that this con had been recently perpetrated on an elderly couple to the tune of several thousand pounds. The husband had since died, but I visited the elderly wife in the presence of her daughter. I showed her an array of photographs. She easily identified Ada as the woman who had demanded VAT from them. Because of the trauma of her recent bereavement, and her obvious frailty, she would not provide me with a statement, which would have enabled me to arrest and charge Ada. But whilst I was chatting to her, and her daughter, there came a knock on the door. The daughter answered and I heard a male voice say,

"The old boy said that he'd pay us to cut the hedge."

I went out into the hallway, identifying myself as a police officer. The man, thick set with a cloth cap perched on his head, retreated to a small pick-up truck parked in the road. In the passenger seat was a small man, whose eyes clearly followed me as I approached.

"Who are you?" I asked the thick set man.

"I'm no one. I don't want anything to do with police."

"Well, who's he then?" indicating the man in the passenger seat.

Oh, don't worry about him. He's blind." I opened the door of the "blind" man to speak to him. The other advanced menacingly on me,

"I knock out coppers," he snarled.

I opened my arms and laughed, "I'm stood here, Do your worst." Swearing to himself, he flopped into the driving seat and drove off.

I'd taken the registration number of the pick-up and, back at the station, I ran a check on it. The two men who were users of the vehicle were well known. Their modus operandi was to offer gardening work on the understanding that the "blind" man be allowed to sit in the victim's house with a glass of water. Whilst the victim was distracted the "blind" man would scour the house, stealing anything of value. Of course, as he'd watched me as I approached their vehicle, it was clear that he wasn't blind at all.

The VAT scam was just one of the arrows in Ada's perverse quiver. She befriended an old man, giving a sob story, tapping him for a loan, to allow her to pay a mortgage that didn't exist. She then visited him numerous times over a five-year period. Once he'd loaned her a substantial sum of money her story changed. She now needed money to allow her to sell the mythical property, to enable her to pay back the loan.

By the time I had contact with this victim, his failing health had confined him to a nursing home. He'd kept a diary of his dealings with Ada. It was obvious from reading the diary that he had no idea why he'd granted the original loan, but once he had, he was snared. To have any hope, however tenuous, of recovering his money, he had to keep loaning more. During that five-year period, he'd loaned Ada over £30,000. Amazingly this man's profession had been accountancy.

Another elderly man was a trustee of his very elderly mother's estate. Somehow, Ada had persuaded him to release tens of thousands of pounds from this estate, giving them to her. She was aided by a man posing as a financial advisor, who had transported the victim and Ada to a solicitor in another town where the transfer of money was made. This is not the last time, in my experience, that solicitors seemed not to have exercised due diligence when handling the affairs of the elderly.

I learned that Ada had begun to victimise an elderly man, who was the sole carer for his disabled wife. I visited the address and to my surprise the door was answered by Ada, whom I recognised from photographs, as at this time I had not had the pleasure of meeting her. It appeared that some months before she had seen the old man struggling with his wheelchair bound wife, and had helped him to get her home. She'd obviously filed him away as a future victim, as she had returned the week before our meeting, and had become indispensable to them.

So indispensable that a solicitor was summoned to arrange a power of attorney on Ada's behalf. She soon began to write cheques drawing on her victim's account. After Ada's arrest and charging, I visited the solicitor practice that arranged the power of attorney. The partner I spoke to was unapologetic. I reported the firm to the Law Society, stating that they had been negligent in not carrying out proper checks on Ada's character. It came as no surprise to me when the Law Society took no action.

You may think that Ada must have lived an opulent lifestyle, fast cars and big houses. Not a bit of it. She was a gambler. I visited many casinos along the South Coast. They were happy to share their records of her losses, this reinforced the incriminating evidence that she was able to use funds that she had no legitimate way of generating. Ada was charged with various offences of deception, receiving a sentence of four years in prison.

At the time I was dealing with Ada I had occasion to speak to a DC from West Yorkshire Police. He was one of three staff that dealt exclusively with the exploitation of elderly and vulnerable people by jobbing builders, or the rag tag people that were their camp followers, like the blind man duo and Ada. He told me that the demand for their services was overwhelming. The offences they uncovered, on a daily basis, were like a giant snowball, gathering volume as it careered downhill, far beyond their capacity to deal with them. I heard, to my amazement, that their squad was being disbanded due to other demands, that their bosses considered more pressing.

It's a cast iron certainty that, nearly thirty years on, this form of offending is still of epidemic proportions. The targets are so easy to victimise. They are so lacking in the ability to defend themselves. They don't want to make a fuss. They believe what they are told by these scumbags, because they have been so honest in their dealings with the world, that can't imagine that someone could stoop to the level of deceit and mendacity that's necessary to perpetrate these crimes.

Any reasonably moral human being will feel disgust at the simple greed and lack of morality of a person that would victimise such vulnerable people. Any illusion that some criminals are like Robin Hood, or Raffles, or the notion that there is any honour amongst thieves, should be discarded without delay. Whether it is the ram raider, or the man that lives by violence, or the man or woman who steals from the vulnerable, they all come from the same drawer. They are lazy, immoral people who want something that someone else has, and don't want to work hard to attain it. Or, they're people that can't suppress their violent, or sexual urges to lead a decent life. As I reported at the beginning of this chapter Anthony Crook hits the bull's eye with his description of criminals as, "A rag bag of useless individuals."

Spare (Fiction)

Mount up! That was the call. That scene is still vivid, despite the accretion of years. We're crammed into the van. Eleven big men on the seats made for small men. Every second is remembered, stretched out, lengthened, like time is being pulled out like a slow-motion film. But the scene turns in on itself, shortens, becomes indistinct. We're not moving. The driver and the Sergeant are out, the Sergeants tunic is unbuttoned, the effect incomplete. We struggle to see, pressing our faces against the perspex screen on the windows, proof against bricks, stones. The old smells, veiled by urgency return to us in our deflation, old farts, stale fags, dirty feet. The electric expectation of the future, our imaginations have conjured for us, fades. All we know is that we're not joining the long column of white vans snaking up the motorway. We're disappointed, cast down.

Although we had never heard of the place, our destination was to have been Orgreave. Orgreave coking plant, South Yorkshire, June 18th 1984. The most violent day of the Miners Strike. The Battle of Orgreave. It was a day that will be remembered in history. History that we should have been part of.

But we weren't.

The Sergeant and the driver are on their hands and knees, intent on some mystery hiding underneath the van. The side door opens, we begin to slowly lever ourselves from our seats, climbing down, standing with our hands in our pockets because we don't know what else to do. Bending our legs self-consciously to peer under the van. Or leaning on the dirty wall of the pit canteen, lighting cigarettes, chewing on crisps, or a green apple from a doggy bag.

One of the rear nearside twin tyres of the van is flat. That's clear. The Sergeant jacks himself to his feet, issuing orders, his energy takes us, energises us, we can still be part of whatever is going on. At his command the metal cradle, holding the spare wheel under the back of the van, is swung down. We view the empty black metal struts of the cradle in disbelief. There is no spare wheel waiting for our eager hands. We speculate idly, because we have nothing else to do. Is the wheel is still leaning against the wall of some workshop hundreds of miles away, or perhaps it never existed at all, It was an idea in the mind of an oil stained mechanic, an idea that dissolved into nothing, as he clocked off, making his way home to his wife and kids. For a long time we stand gormlessly, eyeing the empty cradle, as if by attention alone we can make a wheel appear.

The Sergeant ambles reluctantly away towards the pit office to make a shamefaced telephone call. To confess our ignominy to the world. I slump down on the hard ground, my back against the tired stucco of the canteen wall. It is pleasant to sit there in the summer warmth, not thinking of our uselessness.

"We're in the shit aren't we," I quip to my partner Kev.

"Well, the Sarge is," as he laughs, throwing a small stone at a discarded crisp bag, a free kick wall away. For ten minutes, that's the game. He hits it one more time than me. I'm pissed off at my failure. Forty years later, I still am.

I'm sitting on the step of the van when the Sergeant comes back. Kev is still demonstrating his prowess at hitting a crisp bag with stones. I'm sitting on the step because it feels safe somehow. When it's made whole, this van will transport me back to the army camp where we're quartered, and later safely home to my wife.

"They're a riot going on at a plant where they make coke." The Sergeant imparts as we huddle listlessly around him. None of us want to hear anything more about that. We're missing out. We should be there. "They're sending a mechanic with a spare wheel." His voice was muted, sheepish, he must have taken a beating over the useless van, "There's tea and bacon sandwiches in the canteen."

"Are you in the shit Sarge?" Someone asks.

His laugh is as cold as a December day in Rotherham.

"Always."

The tea is strong, the bacon is fatty. We take our time. Here in Nottinghamshire the canteen staff are all smiles and chat. Most of the local miners chose not to strike. Our purpose being to protect them. A couple of the younger lads are leaning over the counter, flirting with the canteen girls, who giggle and roll their mascaraed eyes. The smell of frying, a radio plays Frankie's

"Two Tribes" in the background, and the hum of the Notts girl's lilt. The walls of the canteen are painted dirty beige. The ceiling is tobacco brown. The Sergeant's head appears at the window, he watches for a moment, but is soon gone.

Later in the bright sunshine and the cloudless sky, I'm alone. There is a hill of slag, that was there when the Great War began, solid, a mountain made by man, and in the distance rolling away, green hills separating the grey uniform pit villages, built only for the mines. There was the sharpness of coal dust in the swaying air, and I felt my redundancy, the feeling that I was out of place, foreign to whatever might happen here.

Later, in the army camp where we're quartered. Over too many pints, we'll hear about the day's events. Our ignominy. It will live with us.

The pit is gone now, housing estates, DIY megastores. The place where we waited for that spare tyre.

Public Order

"Stop, stop!" We shout in unison. There's a disorderly scramble under the seats for our blue NATO riot helmets. Thud, thud, thud, the stones shatter against the sides of the van. We begin to move slowly, forward, the driver picking his way past the wreck of pillaged stone walls, the downed lamp posts.

"Stop!" we scream again. We're all fixed to the rear. A coffee coloured Ford Escort, driven by a Chief Inspector from our Force, is marooned in a sea of attackers, they number, hundreds, swarming the car, the windscreen is gone. Some of them are on the bonnet, one on the roof, wielding a boulder. Down it comes with both hands. Pit boots, heavy shod, kicking, kicking, the car is a mass of panels twisted out of shape, tortured. A bleeding face peers out of the broken and frosted windscreen Eager hands grab, snatch, to drag him out.

We're all out of the van, running, pathetic little pieces of shaped wood in our hands. The Sergeant first, his stick breaks on a man. I remember it clearly. I can still see it from forty years later. They give, even though we are only eleven. Then they surge back a rip tide of stones boots, hate filled faces. But now there are many more of us. The helmet plates of the Greater Manchester Police, red and blue. The dark serge of tunics. The tide ebbs again and is gone. The sorry, coffee coloured car accelerates away up the hill. It's over.

The above is my recollection of a few minutes, perhaps a few seconds, in the early morning sunshine of the 18th June 1984, at Orgreave Coking Plant in South Yorkshire. The Battle of Orgreave, as it became known, was the most controversial day of the year-long mine workers strike of March 1984 to March 1985. Over ninety pickets were arrested that day, being charged with Riot or other serious offences. All were subsequently acquitted due to alleged irregularities in police evidence. It is not my intention to argue the rights and wrongs of what happened that day. After our ordeal on the entrance road, we were kept in reserve in the car park. Most of the controversial incidents, the ones constantly pored over in numerous documentaries and enquiries, played out in a field at the top of the works, or in the village beyond it, in which I, and my colleagues, took no part. What did we do? We sat around on the ground and became very bored, and very hot in the mid-summer sun. A couple of times we were warned to form up to move up to where the action was, but we were soon stood down again. I'll be honest, I was disappointed. I was twenty-five and keen in a naive way to be involved in events, that I sensed, would resonate in history.

The mine worker's strike radically changed the way that British police forces approached the problem of large-scale public disorder. The riots of the early eighties, Brixton in April 1981, and those in other areas of the country, notably Toxteth in Liverpool and Moss Side in Manchester, during the summer of the same year, did highlight the police's lack of appropriate equipment and training in public order. However, the lessons of 1981 were not ingested as thoroughly as they should have been.

My own Force sent officers to Toxteth in July 1981, a year before I joined its ranks. According to veterans of this campaign they were used to guard a pub, at risk from looting, enjoying a very tranquil few days. At training school, a year later, my instruction in public order policing consisted of learning mechanics of a belted cordon, officers grabbed the rear belt of the officer next to them, to provide a barrier to any miscreant, and trudging and wedging, where officers would methodically move forward in a wedge formation to break up a gathering of demonstrators. I remember seeing film from a news helicopter, of the latter tactic being used against a group of pickets during the miner's strike. The wedge broke the mass of pickets, sure, but they simply moved apart and reformed behind the wedging officers. Good in theory, but not in the real world.

Public order. That's what it's called in police jargon. A more fitting description would be public disorder. How the police respond to this disorder, from low level disorder on a Saturday night outside night clubs, right up to full scale riots. My policing experience in the eighties was dominated by public order policing. There were other threats to public order in that decade, such as the policing of New Age Traveller convoys, but I will highlight just two of these. The year-long pit strike already mentioned, and the football violence unleashed in Bournemouth by Leeds United hooligans on the weekend of the 4th to 6th of May 1990, that saw some of the most shocking scenes ever seen at a football match in this country.

When I graduated to operational policing the PSU, Police Support Unit, or riot training consisted of one Sunday a year at HMS Osprey on Portland. The base boasted a concrete village where ships crews practiced fire-fighting. We would shelter behind polycarbonate long shield as instructors threw wooden blocks at us, in the fire blackened mud of the village street, or learn how to extract a violent man from the dark depths of one of the concrete buildings, basically smashing him to the ground using the long shields. Then we'd all troop to the ratings mess and have a very large meal, followed by a couple of pints. As you can guess, we didn't exhibit as much vigour in our afternoon exertions as we had during the morning. All the kit, the shields, the helmets, the thin overalls were all handed back at the end of the day. Nothing was on personal issue. The Force was taking public order training seriously, but not that seriously.

But then came the miner's strike. The strike began in March 1984 after the National Coal Board announced that twenty pits were to close, meaning the loss of 20,000 jobs. The combative President of the National Union of Mineworkers, Arthur Scargill, took up the challenge, calling for a strike. Scargill had pioneered the tactic of "flying pickets," groups of strikers who would descend on a location to "picket," that is to persuade or intimidate workers who wished to work, not to do so. Scargill had achieved success with this tactic at the Saltley Gate fuel depot, near Birmingham, during the 1972 miner's strike.

Scargill refused to call a national ballot of his members, and consequently some mine workers, notably on the Nottinghamshire coalfield, the most profitable in the country, continued to go to work. Aggressive pickets, usually from Scargill's home area of Yorkshire, would descend on these still working Nottinghamshire pits, attempting to intimidate the working miners into going home to spend more time with their families.

The Association of Chief Police Officers had set up the National Reporting Centre in 1972, this body came into its own during the 1984-85 coordinating police activity across the country. Police from forces all over the country were moved into the coalfields to preserve public order, countering the attempts by flying pickets to close down working pits.

Critics of the police tactics during the strike, and there are many, and their publications are legion, claim that police were simply acting as an arm of the government and the Coal Board. Flooding the coalfields with police was intended to undermine the strike for political reasons. Of course, if you sympathise with the aims of the NUM, its easy to come to that conclusion.

One of the more contentious of the tactics used in Nottinghamshire early in the strike, was the practice of turning back flying pickets before they reached the disputed pits. My colleagues and I spent a whole morning on a slip road to the M1 motorway, stopping likely vehicles occupied by brawny men, informing them if they didn't turn back they'd be arrested. The justification for this was, the belief that if these flying pickets were allowed to reach their destination, there would be a breach of the peace. I'll admit that I felt some unease about this at the time, feeling that we were performing more like an occupying army than keepers of the 'Queen's Peace'. The NUM did challenge this tactic in the courts in November 1985, in the case of Moss v McLachlan, but were unsuccessful, as the court found the police action lawful.

The 2009 book by Francis Beckett and David Henke, "Marching to the Fault Line," is typical of the publications that have excoriated police behaviour during the strike. Passages like, "After the first couple of weeks, all over the country, the police attitude toward strikers was cranked up. Strikers suddenly found themselves being treated as enemies of the state......the friendly Bobby turned into a ferocious figure with a horse and a lethal truncheon." Again, I must state that I am only relating my personal experiences. In May 1984 my PSU policed Cotgrave Colliery in Nottinghamshire. All week a group of around ten Derbyshire miners picketed. We grew friendly with them, sharing pork pies and sandwiches, and even engaging in impromptu games of cricket. There is a photograph of some of us with the pickets laughing and cheering.

As Friday afternoon came around, and as we were looking forward to boarding the coach for home, several hundred flying pickets descended from Yorkshire. Our Inspector called for back-up, and soon scores of Met Police arrived in their distinctive green buses. We were pushed to the edge of the cordon thrown around the pickets. A few minutes later the Derbyshire boys worked their way through the crowd to stand with us. I remember one of them declaring, "We've come over to you 'cos we want nothing to do with the fucking Met."

No senior officer ever told us to "crank" up our behaviour. The police response changed to address the increasing violence of the pickets. As the summer of 1984 waned, and miners started to straggle back to work, even in Scargill's heartland of Yorkshire, the focus of the strike changed. Nottinghamshire was a lost cause for the NUM, and we were increasingly deployed to protect miners returning to work on the Yorkshire coalfield.

I remember a week of dark frigid patrols on a wooded hill, overlooking a now forgotten pit. Shining portable searchlights through the misty trees, stamping our feet to stay warm in the Northern frost. The week before pickets had hidden in the woods, before besetting a police van and destroying it. There was no more swopping pies with pickets. No more fun and games. This was deadly serious.

On the 30th November 1984 David Wilkie, a taxi driver, was driving a non-striking miner to work at the Merthyr Vale Colliery in South Wales, when two striking miners dropped a 46 pound concrete block onto his car from a footbridge. Mr Wilkie died at the scene. Two strikers, Russell Shankland and Dean Hancock were convicted of the murder in May 1985, and sentenced to life imprisonment. On appeal the convictions were reduced to that of manslaughter. Both men were released on the 30th November 1989, the fifth anniversary of the death of the unfortunate Mr Wilkie. This death was a grievous blow, not only to the family and friends of David Wilkie, but also to the strike. The support of other trade unionists and the public in general ebbed away. The news that the NUM had received money from the Libyan dictator Colonel Muammar Gaddafi, also tarnished the reputation of Scargill, and his Union. The strike slowly collapsed in the first two months of 1985, Scargill reluctantly calling for a return to work on the 3rd March, his hand forced after a vote for return at a special delegate conference at the TUC in London.

It's difficult to find anybody today who has a good word to say for the Thatcher government's actions during the strike. History has not been kind to her. Again, I have to state that I come from no side about the rights and wrongs of the strike. Since 1985 Britain has de-industrialised. Nearly all deep collieries have closed. Our steel industry is on its last legs, shipbuilding in which we once led the world is gone. Would any of this not happened if the miners had won the strike? Who knows?

But of one thing, I'm sure. The intimidation and violence directed at the miner's who refused to strike was real. The police are sworn to keep the peace, maintain public order. It would not have been possible to simply step back, to allow working miners and their families to be assaulted, their property damaged and their children terrorised. That could not be tolerated in a civilised country.

In early 1990 the Chief Constable of Dorset, Mr Brian Weight, made a request to the Football League to reschedule the Division Two game between AFC Bournemouth and Leeds United. The fixture was set to be played during the Bank Holiday weekend, on the 5th May 1990. The Yorkshire side had a well deserved reputation for attracting a hooligan element amongst their supporters, and Mr Weight, rightly, as it turned out, concluded that a long hot weekend on the South Coast would attract the worst of these elements. To make matters worse the match was a vital one for both sides. If Leeds won, they would be automatically promoted to the First Division, if Bournemouth lost, they would be relegated to the Third. The football authorities refused to switch the fixture. The rest is history, some of the worst football violence seen in this country.

By this time, I was a Sergeant at Wareham Police Station. On Friday 4th May I was rostered to work a late shift as a Sergeant on a PSU, made up of officers from outside the Poole/Bournemouth conurbation. Our duties were to monitor football supporters in Bournemouth town centre. As we arrived it was clear that there were a large number of Leeds supporters already there, probably several hundred. Two PSUs are made up of forty constables, four sergeants and two inspectors. Not enough to control the situation if the shit hit the fan.

The weather was good, but bad for us, sunny, drinking weather. We were stood by in a turning circle adjacent to Bournemouth International Centre. The conurbation PSU was at Bournemouth Police Station having a meal. That means we numbered twenty-three. In front of us the road sloped down to a flyover in front of the Pier. Near the flyover, and to the left of it was the Bournemouth Pavilion. At the rear of the Pavilion, nearest to us, was a bar. It appeared that a great many Leeds supporters were in that bar and outside, chanting, and making a great deal of noise. Then suddenly, there was a loud crash, the supporter began to stream out of the bar, someone had set fire to a motorbike outside. Welcome to mayhem.

Our Inspector, Martin Jones, immediately ordered us out of our vans to form a cordon across the road on the flyover. He in front, then the Sergeants, then the PCs spread out behind. By this time there were at least a hundred Leeds hooligans on the flyover facing us and they were in a very frisky mood, oiled by gallons of beer. We were in shirt sleeves wearing our ordinary helmets, and I remember feeling very vulnerable as the first full beer can came hurtling over, followed by a lot more. The beer cans smacked against the road and exploded into froth. Martin Jones ordered us to produce our truncheons, to brandish them at the hooligans, showing that we meant business. There's a photograph, taken from behind us. We're facing up the hill, truncheon in our hands, facing the mob. After the weekend was over a team of detectives was set up to pursue the Leeds supporters who were not arrested on the day. The exercise was dubbed Operation Boar Hunt. That photograph was theatrically dubbed, "The Thin Blue Line," by the Boar Hunt Team.

But that was in the future. On that evening we were in trouble. The Leeds yobs had clearly taken in our lack of numbers, as the beer cans began to fly thick and fast. Martin Jones was struck on the hand. He swore explosively as the can shattered and frothed on the road. They were moving closer. I remember debating to myself if I would run away or not, as if they attacked as we were clearly going to get the shit kicked out of us. I swear they were about to charge when blue lights appeared behind them. The other PSU had left their half-eaten dinners on the table, speeding back to come to our aid. The Leeds fans filtering away into Bournemouth Gardens, like a swiftly ebbing tide.

For the rest of the evening we followed them around the town centre. A few were arrested, but our main objective was to split them up, keep them on the move, so that they couldn't use their numbers to overwhelm us. I trusted that the Force was mobilising more PSUs, as we sorely needed them.

As it began to get dark my serial, a serial is half a PSU, that is ten PCs, under the command of a sergeant, found ourselves shepherding a group of around fifty yobs from the town centre, through a subway into the gardens. By this time we'd put on our NATO riot helmets, and carried round polycarbonate shields. As I went down into the subway someone threw a full can of Carlsberg Special Brew from above, shattering on my NATO helmet and covering me in frothy beer. There was no way that I could identify who did it, so we continued to push the group out into the open gardens, near the Bourne stream, that runs through the gardens to the sea. I smelled strongly of beer for the rest of the night.

Suddenly, as if in one mind, sensing that they outnumbered us five to one, the group turned and attacked us. Stupid move. Soon they were put to flight at the point of our truncheons. I felled one man, wearing a white Leeds shirt, with a blow to his body. It's difficult to explain how a man reacts in that situation. The adrenalin is up and, although you are a peacekeeper, you're in combat mode. My first instinct was to hit him again, but he raised his arms defensively in front of him as I raised my stick, the blow was stayed. "Now, Fuck off!" I spat, as he struggled to his feet and ran off after his mates. Later that evening we were relieved by fresh officers, but were told to be back in the morning.

The next morning, we trailed at low speed up the long Holdenhurst Road, from the town centre to Bournemouth's Dean Court ground in the town's King's Park. Many of the shops along the road had suffered broken windows in the wake of the Leeds mob.

A great many of the Leeds supporters had travelled without a match ticket. In those days the ground was small by many standards, and there was no way that they could gain entry to watch the game. The ground had a large gravel and broken ground car park around it, and beyond a road that that bisected King's Park, were playing fields and cricket pitches. The Force had been busy, as by this time there were a very large number of police in the vicinity of the ground. Mutual aid from surrounding forces, mounted police from the City of London. From around midday, until kick off at three, we made repeated charges to clear hooligans, who had been pelting us with stones and any other debris from the car park, out onto the road and onto the cricket pitches. I found our tactics inexplicable, as,when we'd cleared them, senior officers ordered us back to the ground allowing the Leeds yobs to close in on us again, rather them keeping them on the grass where there was no ammunition. We must have done this five or six times. At one point a uniformed St John's Ambulance Brigade Member became mixed up with the mob. They set about him for no apparent reason, leaving him broken on the stony ground, until we again surged forward to rescue him.

At 3pm hostilities were suspended, the Leeds mob listening to the game on transistor radios. It was a very warm day and we stood confronting the now static crowd until five. Leeds won the game, propelling them into the top league, consigning Bournemouth to obscurity in Division Three. We spent the whole evening chasing celebrating supporters, engaged in all sorts of damage and mayhem, around the town.

Football violence was a disease that afflicted the game in England during the seventies and eighties. Although it's not totally gone away, the 1989 Hillsborough disaster, when 97 supporters were crushed to death during an FA Cup semi-final in Sheffield, was the watershed moment. The report by Lord Justice Taylor into the disaster, recommended all seater stadiums. This recommendation was accepted, being implemented swiftly by football authorities. This along with a definite, but difficult to define, change in culture, virtually eradicated football related violence.

Public disorder is generated by a myriad of causes. From national industrial disputes, to a couple of drunks swinging haymakers at each other late on a Saturday night. Police are often caught in the middle of situations with complex origins, many outside the ability of the police to affect. As Professor Robert

Reiner observes in his excellent "Politics and the Police," "With the conditions of civility eroded, the watchman keeps watch in vain.'"

Arson (Fiction)

The darkness has already come down as the boy locked the door of the cafe. He can hear the sea, but tonight it's different. There's something that he doesn't recognise, a depth, a thickness, that is new to him. He stands for a while to let it come into him, the long roll of the strangeness of it. He pulls the door to him again, to check. An unease grips him unlike anything he's felt before, as if he's unsure of the nature of the ocean filling behind him, or the black shape of the cliff crowding ahead of him. The air has the scent of distant burning. He senses that tonight is the night.

Coming around the side of the squatting building he sees him in the rising light of the moon. Sitting on the bonnet of his small white car, with the piddling black light on the roof that he knew was blue, and the badge on the door, just visible, then vivid in the headlamps of a passing car, purring slowly down the beach road. Purple and silver, and a crown.

The man has the look of a prop forward. The helmet on his head is black, the badge glinting at angles, his arms folded patiently across the front of his bulging pale shirt. He is silent tonight. At least he does not speak, but the static is strong.

He had been there first four nights since. It was the boy's turn to lock up for the week. He was alone for the last half hour or so. Washing, tidying, mopping down. On the first night the boy had spoken to the man, "Goodnight." The silence that was his reply had seemed comical to him then. He'd laughed out loud, mocking, as he climbed into his car, driving up the hill to the beach road. But he'd been careful to look in his mirror. The man had not moved, as if his place in the world was set, and there was no altering it.

The following night the man was smoking a cigarette. He smelt it as he turned the key in the lock. He'd thought for a moment that one of his friends was waiting to take him for a drink before last orders. He was cheered, as he'd been fighting a feeling of dread, a feeling that had been slowly eddying around him all day. The tip of the man's cigarette glowed as he came into sight, sitting, exactly as he had the night before. No words were exchanged as he passed to his car, but the man's eyes were like blocks of deeper obsidian under the dark brow of his helmet.

In his head he saw the car burning. How he'd stayed as close as he could, relishing the power that he had. Then retreating into the darkness as people spilled out of the houses, almost as if they'd come to admire his work.

He looked out on the third night. He considered calling his Father, he thought of calling to make a police complaint. He realized, with a sickening finality, that he could do neither. As the time came for leaving, he was drawn to the man, as if a supplicant to a king.

"What have you done?" The man said. His voice was deep, local edged, with a sonorous depth, that spoke of something beyond the boy's understanding. That night he had not replied but looked instead to the thinning horizon, burning reds and purples and pinks, like that night.

So, tonight, the fourth night, it must end. The road winds up the hill and away towards the town. He's known that road all his life but tonight his eyes are drawn to it, and it seems to him to have some special place, some unique significance in what is to come.

The back door of the man's car is open, and he knows that his life will never regain the significance, the pride, that he has placed in it. His voice is low, but clear, in the still air of the dark cove, enclosed by the cliffs and sea, as he stands before the man.

"I'm the one that did it. I'm the one you want.

"I Want to Complain About PC Smith"

I'd tried to get out of this as I was in the last year or before my retirement. But all my efforts had been in vain. "Everyone has to do it," my boss told me. Everyone. A seminar for supervisors, every April. When the Chief Constable explained his policing plan for the coming year, how we all had to strive to achieve his targets. One year a colleague of mine, who'd been having domestic problems at the time, had fallen asleep in the front row. "Is that man ill?" The Chief bellowed, pointing at my unfortunate colleague. An apology had been offered, after the Chief's riveting homily, and all was well.

This particular year, the gathering took place at a hall on an industrial park adjacent to Headquarters. The Police Authority had appointed a new Assistant Chief Constable from an adjacent force. She chaired the meeting, and clearly had a bee in her bonnet about complaints. Complaints by members of the public against police. Our Force had a higher than average level of complaints per capita than most other forces, and it was her assertion that this was unacceptable.

This was early 2012. Complaints are generally recorded by inspectors, who have the responsibility for early investigation and securing the initial evidence, photographing injuries, seizing CCTV footage, making initial approaches to witnesses etc. I'd been taking complaints since 1992 when I began acting inspector duties, hundreds of complaints. Most weren't complaints at all. People just wanted someone to show some interest in their problems.

One of the main difficulties with this is that when someone called the call centre, uttering the word "complaint," the call taker would head the computer log with that word "Complaint," sending it to the duty inspector without any clear idea of what a police complaint is. A good example is Mrs Brown calls and tells me, "PC Smith said he'd call me on Monday about my case, and she hasn't." Fine. Quite legitimate to bring PS Smith's supervisors attention to this, as PC Smith had made a commitment that they'd failed to carry out. Of course, PC Smith might have forgotten, they might have been committed guarding a crime scene for their entire shift, they may have been sick on that day. In response to this I would apologise on PC Smith's behalf, contacting the officer, making sure that they telephoned the complainant the next time they were on duty, or I would want to know why. Mrs Brown would now think that Inspector Hicks was a top-notch bloke, and even PC Smith wasn't that bad. You see, in my experience Mrs Brown, and thousands like her, don't expect miracles from the police. Most people are quite realistic about the world, not expecting a combination of Sherlock Holmes and CSI Miami when someone kicks their car door mirror off. They just want to feel that the police care about their situation, and will do all they can to make it right. A Section Commander, an Inspector in charge of a station, who I worked with, produced a brochure for his staff telling them what he expected of them. The one phrase in it, that I'll always remember, is that he entreated his men and women to be "unfailingly interested" in the problems of people calling on them for help. That has stuck with me, because I think its genius. That is what the public want. That's what the police should be giving them.

 So, what had this to do with our new ACC and her chagrin at our complaint numbers? I took and initially investigated complaints for twenty years. I got quite good at it. At a seminar for inspectors in 2010 I was singled out by the Head of Professional Standards as the most efficient officer in the Force, when it came to recording and completing the initial investigation of such matters. Okay, big headed bastard, you may say. But praise in this life is so rare that you should crow about it when you get it. Most takers of complaints are not so experienced, and will record virtually anything. PC Lear looked at me in a sexist way when I was arrested for kerb crawling. PC Carrot was uncomplimentary about my allotment when someone unlawfully lifted my spuds. PC Skidmark made an uncomplimentary remark about my driving when my car ended up in a hedge. Okay, I exaggerate, but only slightly. We record too much utter dross as complaints, but a skilful supervisor can turn that complaint into a plus for public relations, if they're switched on in the right way.

My hand went up at that supervisors meeting in 2012, I couldn't help myself. "Ma'am," I proclaimed, "The reason why our complaints totals are so high, is that we record utter rubbish as complaints, as most supervisors have no idea how to sift these out, as they receive no training. This is the fault of the Force." She looked at me for a few seconds, as if I was some creature that had just crawled out of a dark lake, or just landed from Mars sporting two heads, then turned away and continued with her prepared talk. This particular lady was soon promoted to Deputy Chief, then Chief Constable, luckily by that time, I had long retired.

I'm the first to acknowledge that police get it badly wrong sometimes. I also acknowledge that there are people that are bad and should never be police officers, those who occasionally beat the vetting and assume the privileges and powers of an officer, when they do not have the integrity that is necessary to perform that office. Recent horrendous examples, such as Wayne Couzens, who sexually assaulted and murdered Sarah Everard, and in my own Force, PC Tim Brehmer, who killed Claire Parry a woman that he had been having an affair with in 2020. I knew Brehmer and would never have believed that he was capable of such an act. These are extreme examples, but I also know of police officers that were drug dealers, officers that engaged in mortgage fraud, stole money from old people after they had become victims of crime. But I know of them because they were caught, went to prison, and were fired.

For your entertainment I'll just run through a few of the more amusing complaints that I dealt with over the years. In around 2009 I received a call log that was restricted. Only I and Professional Standards could access it. It alleged that the caller had information about serious police corruption in my force. I visited the complainant who was a disabled man of around thirty years of age. He was bedridden and my heart went out to him, but I wondered how he could have learned of serious corruption. I asked him to relate to me what he knew. Unfortunately, he could only talk in very general terms of his perception of the corruption of all UK police, he knew that, "British police are the most corrupt in the world." Before I left I assured him that I would relay his concerns to our Professional Standards Department. I mused on what he'd told me on the way back to the station, on how officers in our provincial force could be more corrupt than Mexican police, who actively collude with drug cartels, running kidnapping and extortion rackets, or Kenya, where suspects, victims of extortion and human rights lawyers are routinely murdered by police. Or Pakistan, where police have colluded with the military to jail the democratically elected Prime Minister, Imran Khan, on trumped up charges to prevent him running in an election. Often, I think that Britons have lived all their lives in such a cosseted environment, that they have little perception of the real evil that lurks out there in the world.

A dowdy looking woman in her early thirties came to me one day to complain that the officer dealing with her complaint of misuse of her bank cards had discussed her sex life with the offender. I spoke to PC X who was dealing with the case. She readily admitted that this was the case because it was relevant. The lady had omitted to inform me that she was a dominatrix, the offender being her "Gimp." That's why he had access to her bank cards and her pin numbers. When I reinterviewed the lady, she told me that she hadn't mentioned this as many people were, "judgemental," about her "alternative" lifestyle.

We'll call him Christopher Green. He was, and still is, a reprehensible, vile character. I had most dealings with him in the nineties and early two thousands. He was a thief, a sex offender and violent. His speciality act was as a Peeping Tom. He was continually arrested and convicted for all sorts of offences, but seemed to stay out of prison most of the time, this speaks volumes for our toothless criminal justice system. When he was arrested, he invariably made complaints against the arresting officers, quite often he alleged assault, as his habit was to violently resist arrest.

One dark evening Green was detained by residents of a block of flats, as he had peered in through a ground floor at a young girl undressing in her bedroom. They were, understandably in my opinion, not gentle with him. When he arrived at the police station he was bleeding heavily from a wound to the top of his head. I was informed that he wanted to make a complaint, alleging the arresting officers had inflicted the wound on him. I saw him in an interview room. By this time the blood had dried and covered his face like a red mask. He had refused to wash it off.

He'd been charged and kept in custody for court the next morning. We did sensible things like that in those days. We sat opposite each other, he glaring at me.

"When the court sees me tomorrow, they'll see just what you bastards have done to me." He snarled. We were old friends me and him, very familiar with each other, so I decided to be honest with him.

"When the magistrates see you in that state tomorrow, do you know what they're going to think Christopher?"

He looked at me quizzically through his rust-coloured mask, "What will they think?"

"They'll think, that this man is a complete cunt."

He eyed me like an animal who'd seen a human for the first time. His face seemed to twist and turn as if he was wrestling with great questions.

After a time he said, "Yes, they may think that." He got up, "I want to go back to my cell now." I understand that he did wash his face before going to court the next morning.

Armed Police!

It was the 3rd April 1993, I remember that date because it was the day of the, "The Grand National that never was." The race, at Aintree in Liverpool, had been declared void, as there'd been a false start, but many of the competitors had carried on, thundering down the course anyway. The race was never re-run. It was sometime in mid-afternoon. It'd been raining heavily, but the downpour had now abated, rivers of water pouring away into the roadside drains. I'm the Acting Inspector on a day shift, due to finish at five. I'm driving alone, intending to visit one of the three police stations that are my responsibility. The radio comes to life, "Burglary in progress at X dairy." I'm less than five minutes away. I'm in an unmarked car so I pick my way slowly through traffic. Then a call from control room, a firearm is seen by a witness. The armed response vehicle is alerted, and is en route. I can hear the sirens in the background as they acknowledge the call. A garbled message, a firearm has been discharged at Fleetsbridge roundabout, I'm one minute away. I force my way past the queuing traffic, take in the scene as I fall from my car.

A marked police Ford Sierra, stationary, half on half off the pavement at right angles to the traffic. A lone female officer looking into the car. The front passenger window of the car shattered. In shock I approach the car, two bloodied bodies lay in the front seats, two men I know well, friends. The female officer is shouting into her radio, calling for an ambulance. She's very calm, professional, I remember that.

The officer sitting up stiffly in the passenger seat has lacerations to his left leg, his trousers ripped open. The driver, slumped down behind the wheel, is wounded to his left side, from his head down his arm and into his body. He's the worst of the two, in a bad way. I'm on the radio directing the ARV, doing what I can, pretending I'm in charge, but in reality, the control room is doing all the work. The officer shot in the leg is walking wounded, he's out of the car. I help to lever the driver out, carrying him as gently as can be to the ambulance.

Both officers recovered, eventually returning to duty. Both suffered severe mental trauma during their recovery and later, some of which I witnessed, but the long-term effects on them, I can only guess at.

It appears that they'd blocked the entrance to the roundabout to the suspect vehicle, a stolen Ford Sierra Cosworth, a top-notch speed wagon at the time. A robber had simply wound down his window, letting fly with a shotgun without warning. The officer on the passenger side, seeing what was about to happen, squeezed his body down into the footwell, leaving his leg exposed, but allowing the car door to protect his body. The driver couldn't take any evasive action, taking the full blast of the shot, his foot slipping off the clutch, lurching the Sierra forward and up onto the footpath. The bandit car had maneuvered by and away. The car was later recovered abandoned. It had been torn apart during forensic examination, but nothing was found. No arrests were ever made.

When dispatched to the incident the ARV had only been between five to ten minutes away, but even this was too far for any meaningful intervention. I'll come back to this point later.

In my medium sized town, 1993 was the year of the gun. In addition to the events I've described, a double crewed police car was sent to a report of a firearm lying on top of a post box, late at night, on an estate that housed a number of troublesome criminals. As the two officers slowed up to examine the post box, someone opened fire on them with a hand-gun, shots thumping into the car, but not, thankfully the two officers. I was told that a world record was set in the category of reversing. For a time no call to that estate could be responded to without the attendance of an armed response vehicle.

Later, in the summer of the year, a robbery occurred at a post office near the same estate, a robber with a shotgun, riding pillion on a motorbike. As the robber burst from the doorway of the post office, a courageous member of the public attempted to intervene, but was shot in the leg for his troubles. As the motorcycle roared away, an off duty Royal Marine, from a base nearby, rammed it with his car, sending the riders smashing through the large display window of the tiny shop. Both robbers limped off on foot. One, the rider of the motorbike, not the shooter, was caught skulking behind a gravestone in a nearby cemetery. The identity of the shooter was soon known. He was speedily arrested.

The two robbers were placed in a cell together before charge, a most irregular occurrence. They clearly didn't appreciate the unusual nature of this arrangement, as they proceeded to chat excitedly about their recent exploits, like a pair of plastic gangsters. Unbeknownst to them, the Chief Constable had authorised that the cell be wired for sound. This he was permitted to do, before the hugely bureaucratic Regulation of Investigatory Powers Act of 2000 became law to complicate matters. These boastful admissions went a long way to ensuring the men's convictions, and the imposition of very lengthy prison sentences. Incidentally, on emerging from prison, both men were soon behind bars again, after committing more serious offences. Advocates for alternative sentences to prison, will point to this as a failure of the deterrent effect of custody. I would point to the fact that neither committed any offences, causing anguish and harm to the law abiding, while they were locked up.

These long sentences did seem to choke off the rise in armed robbery, in the force area, for a while. But madmen aren't deterred by the prospect of prison time. One night a year or so after these events, I was out on patrol with a PC in a car. Early on our night shift, at around 11-30pm, the control room directed us to a nearby social club where a robbery was in progress. That's all the information we were given. We raced to the scene, leaving our car to block the entrance of the car park, we burst into the building, little wooden truncheons raised menacingly above our heads. The two women in the club told us that the robber had just left, a fact that filled us with relief, as they added that he'd been armed with a sawn-off shotgun!

One of the ladies, who lived on an estate nearby, told us that the robber had been wearing a back to front balaclava, with eye slits cut in it. Through these slits, she'd seen a pair of bushy ginger eyebrows. She recognized these eyebrows as belonging to an ex-soldier, an inveterate criminal, who lived near to her. This man was known to be mentally unhinged and very violent. For a time, he was suspected of being the gunman, who had taken the pot shots at the police car a year or so before. On hearing this my colleague and I were doubly glad that we'd arrived too late, very ill equipped to confront a lunatic with a shotgun.

On his arrest, by armed officers of course, there was no trace of the shotgun, the balaclava, or any of the few hundreds of pounds of cash that he'd grabbed, before disappearing into the night. He agreed to an identification parade, all of the participants wearing balaclavas I didn't witness this, so can't speak to the extent of other participants in the parade's gingerness. The lady from the club picked the crook out without difficulty. Success you may say. Unfortunately, the Crown Prosecution Service declined to prosecute, based on the absence of other evidence.

Incidentally, at training school, one bright afternoon in September 1982, during a self-defence lesson, the Sergeant Instructor gave up some sage advice on what to do when confronted by a criminal with a firearm.

"When addressing this situation, you must take the correct steps. Bloody big ones in the opposite direction!"

Cops aren't supermen. Live to nick the bastard another day.

When I was a PC, in the eighties, I applied for firearms training. I was accepted, but before I could attend the course, I was promoted to sergeant. The rule at the time was, no sergeant could carry a firearm, unless they'd done so as PC. So, apart from firing a Sig Sauer pistol, and a Heckler and Koch MP5 on a firearms familiarisation course as an Inspector, I was never to carry a firearm whilst a police officer.

It's pretty much taken as an everyday occurrence nowadays, that members of the public will see heavily armed police officers at airports, at Parliament, Downing Street, see armed response vehicles speeding by, filled with black overalled, paramilitary style officers, tooled up with pistols, rifles, baton guns and other less lethal weaponry. When Peel's first officers set out on patrol in 1829, they were emphatically denied firearms, as this would have been a barrier between them and the public they served. They were merely citizens in uniform. Terrorism is obviously one of the main drivers prompting the option of armed police, available 24 hours a day. It's fascinating to observe how the current situation developed, I'll try to explain how this happened.

I'm indebted to Michael J. Waldren's fascinating 2007 book, "Armed Police. The Police Use of Firearms since 1945." It deals mainly with the Metropolitan Police, but gives trenchant insights into how we got here. Of course, what happens in the country's largest and most famous force, has always had profound implications for forces all over the country.

It would not be accurate to say that Peel's police were totally denied firearms in 1829. Records show that the force bought fifty pairs of flintlock pistols in that year, for use on patrol. Two police officers were shot and killed in early 1880s, leading for calls to arm all officers. A vote in favour of arming, by Metropolitan officers, prompted the Commissioner to concede that officers could carry a firearm on night duty, if they could be "trusted to use them with discretion."

Throughout the first half of the twentieth century firearms were carried on protection duty, or when escorting bullion. They were also issued for the arrest of a criminal who was known to carry a firearm.

In 1965, the death penalty for murder was effectively abolished. The Murder (Abolition of Death Penalty) Act, saw the penalty suspended for five years. Capital punishment was finally abolished in 1969.

On the 12th August 1966, Harry Roberts, John Duddy and John Witney, all convicted, habitual criminals, were on the prowl, in a scruffy 1954 Vanguard estate car, outside Wormwood Scrubs prison in Shepherd's Bush, London. The trio were looking for a car to steal, to use later in a robbery. Three police officers, DS Christopher Head, DC David Wombwell and PC Geoffrey Cox, in a "Q car," an unmarked police car, were patrolling in the area. The officers observed the Vanguard as it loitered in an area near the prison, from which there had been a number of escape attempts in recent months. As DC Wombwell and DS Head approach the Vanguard on foot, Roberts shot DC Wombwell in the face without warning, killing him instantly. DS Head quickly retreated, but Roberts shot him in the back, severely wounding him. Roberts fired again, but his gun jammed. Duddy took his place, firing an old .38 service revolver at PC Fox, the driver of the Q car. The first two rounds missed, but the third hit Fox in the temple, ending his life. The unfortunate officer's foot jammed down on the accelerator, lurching the Q car forward, running over, and killing DS Head. This heinous slaughter would have definitely attracted the death penalty, for all three offenders, prior to its suspension in 1965. Outraged voices, both citizens and police, called for its return, as an appropriate response to this atrocity. This terrible incident went some way to changing the manner in which police used and trained to use firearms. It was to be over a decade before the Met police set up its first dedicated firearms team, designated as D11, and over twenty years before the first armed response vehicles appeared on the streets. But it was in 1966 that it became clear that police would have to professionalise its approach in the field of firearms. The period immediately after the murders, and particularly the time when Roberts was run to ground in Epping Forest, exposed the lackadaisical, almost farcical police approach to firearms handling. PC Tony Gray was stationed at Kingston Police Station. His entire shift had been called in to search for Roberts. He relates,

"When the Sergeant asked us whether anybody had experience with revolvers, I said that I had. I had been in the armoured corps in the army and in the fifties you trained on a Webley. You fired it once a year, and as long as you heard it go bang, or saw a photograph of someone who had, then you were qualified."

At this the Sergeant produced a revolver which was wrapped in greaseproof paper, it had never been issued before, telling PC Gray, "Don't you load it whatever you do, but most importantly don't you bloody well use it on anybody."

Even before Roberts was arrested, in Thorley Woods, Hertfordshire, on the 12th November 1966, the Commissioner of the Metropolitan Police, Sir Joseph Simpson, had decided to radically overhaul the training of officers in firearms use. Each authorised officer should be properly trained, receive a refresher course every four months, and have to re-qualify every year.

The history of the police use of firearms seems to be run through with a common theme. That is, that senior officers recognised the need for some officers to be routinely armed, but they were reluctant to take the further step to allow this to happen. In the late sixties and early seventies there was a spate of armed robberies connected to Christmas Club payout days. Senior officers grudgingly agreed to the issue of firearms to combat this, but then added the ludicrous caveat that these weapons could not be carried whilst loaded.

In the early seventies Irish terrorism came to the streets of mainland Britain. On the 22nd February 1972 the IRA detonated a bomb at the headquarters of the army's 16th Parachute Brigade in Aldershot, in retaliation, the terrorists claimed, for the shootings in Londonderry on the 30th January of that year, known as Bloody Sunday. The Aldershot bomb claimed the lives of 7 civilian workers, including five women, a gardener and a Roman Catholic priest. London was the main target for attacks in the early seventies, including the Old Bailey bomb in March 1973, that injured 162 innocent people. On the 22nd January 1975 PC Stephen Tibble, who was off duty, saw police chasing a man in Baron's Court, West London. The man was William Quinn, an American IRA volunteer. As PC Tibble crouched to tackle Quinn, the terrorist produced a firearm and fired three times, striking and killing the gallant officer. Quinn was later arrested in San Francisco, where he spent five years fighting extradition. In 1988, At the Old Bailey he was sentenced to life imprisonment for the murder of PC Tibble.

Three months after the Murder of Stephen Tibble The Metropolitan Police set up its first full time firearms team. This team was primarily to be trained to confront terrorists, who may have taken hostages, and barricaded themselves into buildings. These teams would be used in situations where, "A highly trained team, expert in the use of a wide range of firearms would be necessary." This team could also be used in cases of serious armed crime. The team would have its own transport and would make use of pistols, rifles, sub-machine guns, shotguns and the latest body armour.

This team was soon called into action. On the 28th September 1975, an armed robbery, at the Spaghetti House restaurant in Knightsbridge, turned into a siege, when unarmed police quickly arrived on the scene. Nine hostages were held in the basement of the restaurant. The team was deployed, and the area contained. No concessions were made to the robbers, who, after six days, surrendered without harming the hostages. The only bloodshed occurred when the leader of the gang, Franklin Davies, a Nigerian student, shot himself in the stomach. He later recovered from his wounds and was jailed for twenty-two years. The armed containment was deemed by all to be a great success. The efficient containment and surrender of a heavily armed IRA cadre, at Balcombe Street, NW1, in December 1975, cemented the reputation of the team, even amongst senior officers who still harboured doubts.

The shooting of Stephen Waldorf, by non-team armed officers, on the 14th January 1983, was a public relations disaster for the Metropolitan Police, but was a further spur towards the complete professionalisation in the sphere of the police use of firearms. Waldorf had been shot whilst a passenger in a Mini car at Pembroke Road, Earl's Court. Officers mistook Waldorf for a dangerous wanted man, David Martin, who was wanted for the attempted murder, by shooting, of a police officer. The vehicle had been under surveillance, as it was being used by Martin's girlfriend, Sue Stephens. Waldorf was seriously injured but survived. Two officers stood trial for attempted murder, and inflicting grievous bodily harm on Waldorf, but were acquitted. The Met paid substantial damages to Waldorf, along with a smaller sum to Stephens.

Following this public relations disaster, Sir Geoffrey Dear, one of the HM Inspectors of Constabulary, was asked to chair a working party on the selection and training of firearms officers. The Dear report was finalised in December 1983, recommending psychological tests in firearms office selection, increased intensity and length of training and improved tactical instruction. This allied to the publication of the ACPO "Manual of Guidance on Police Use of Firearms," thoroughly professionalised and standardised firearms tactics and training throughout the country.

On the 19th August 1987, twenty-seven year old Michael Ryan shot and killed sixteen people, in and around the small town of Hungerford, Berkshire. The victims included his own mother and an unarmed police officer. Ryan arsenal included a Beretta pistol, an M1 carbine and a Type 56 rifle, a Chinese version of the infamous AK47. Ryan began the killing in the Savernake Forest in Wiltshire, where he shot and killed a young woman picnicking with her small children. He then moved on to nearby Hungerford, where he murdered another fifteen people. Later in the day Ryan ended his own life by shooting himself in the temple.

As a result of this massacre, ownership of certain types of firearms were prohibited. But it was the McLachlan Report, the inquiry into the events at Savernake and Hungerford, that was to have the most far-reaching impact. As Michael J. Waldren observes, "This (the McLachlan Report,) examined the police response to the incident .... but the greatest amount of space was taken up with the merits of armed response vehicles." Had there been an ARV, as they became known, in the area of Hungerford on that fateful day in August 1987, Ryan's terrible rampage may have been interrupted and many lives saved.

From the late eighties onwards ARVs operated in Dorset and every other force in the country. Because of the need for high powered vehicles, for fast response, the first ARV officers in Dorset were drawn exclusively from the Traffic Division, who were advanced driver trained. These officers were part time Traffic, part time ARV. This changed as the nineties wore on, allowing more officers to be trained in, not only in firearms handling and tactics, but also in advanced driving. By 1998 the force made the decision to set up a full time ARV department. This was quite a commitment, forty PCs, along with supervisors.

One final word about ARVs. When the two officers were shot at the roundabout in 1993, as described at the opening of this chapter, the ARV was less than five minutes away from this awful scene. They burned tyres to get there, but still didn't affect the outcome. The armed response vehicle is a half-way house to the complete arming of British police. Its ability to affect the situation in spontaneous incidents is limited.

Given the current state of the country it's very unlikely, that British police will ever divest themselves of firearms, returning to a more tranquil time, when all officers could patrol unarmed.

I'll leave the final word to Michael J. Waldren, whose authoritative book I am indebted to for this chapter. Speaking of the Shepherd's Bush murders he writes,

"What gives pause for thought is the realisation that, despite all the developments since that horrific crime so many years ago, it could happen again tomorrow. The police service faces the first half of the twenty-first century with absolutely no idea of just how much it may still have to change."

Postscript

As I dot the final full stop in this chapter, on the 21st October 2024, in a trial at the Old Bailey, Sergeant Martyn Blake of the Metropolitan Police is found not guilty of the murder of Chris Kaba, in September 2022. It emerged after the trial that Kaba, 24, who had been portrayed as a family-oriented rap artist, and a would be architect, was actually a violent gang member, who boasted a string of convictions for violence, despite his relatively tender years. He'd shot a rival gang member in a night club in Hackney, just six days before his own death.

On that night he'd been driving an Audi Q8 in Streatham, South London, when he'd been the subject of a stop by armed officers. The vehicle he'd been driving was used in a shooting the night before in Brixton. Kaba's vehicle had been boxed in by police vehicles and he'd attempted to ram these vehicles out of the way to facilitate his escape, violently ramming backwards and forwards, recklessly crashing into the encircling police vehicles. Sergeant Blake, who was positioned at the front of Kaba's vehicle, fearing that an officer would be run over and killed, fired one shot wounding Kaba, who later died in hospital.

Unbelievably, given the circumstances, the CPS made the decision to charge the officer with murder. Under pressure from the press, most notably the BBC and the Guardian, of course, Judge Mark Lucraft ruled in March 2024, that the involved officer should be publicly named because,

"In my judgment the naming the defendant or in giving his date of birth does not give rise to a real and immediate risk to his life."

It in unknown on what evidence Lurcraft based his assessment. A Met Police intelligence report cast doubt on the learned Judge's assessment when it concluded that,

"The likelihood of consequences following the identification of the officer is very high. The threat to the officer and their family in the event they are identified is very high" Supt Ross McKibbin, head of Counter Terrorism in the Met observed,

"In nearly 30 years of service, I have never been more concerned about the welfare of an officer or the likelihood of them or their family coming to serious harm, as I am about Martyn Blake in this case."

It was revealed during the trial that London gangs had offered a bounty of £10,000 for any person that carried out the murder of Sergeant Blake, or any member of his family. He, along with his wife and children, have been forced to go into hiding, with close police protection. He could still face gross misconduct proceedings that could result in him losing his job, a job that it's probably impossible for him to return to anyway.

Why would any police officer wish to carry a firearm today? Every excuse seems to be made for armed criminals, giving them an immense latitude, a wide avenue to transgress the law, without being challenged on account of their behaviour. But on the rare occasions when police discharge a firearm, resulting in the death, or injury, of a violent criminal, the officer and their family face years of repeated enquiries and second guessing by the IOPC, the CPS, inquests, and even public enquiries.

The case of Azelle Rodney, perfectly illustrates the incredible scrutiny that any discharge of police firearms receives, and the resulting years of uncertainty that officers and their families face.

On the 30th April 2005 Azelle Rodney, who was later described as a mid-level criminal, and at the time of this incident was wanted by police in connection with two stabbing incidents, was riding in a car in Barnet, North London, with two other men, when it was stopped by firearms officers of the Metropolitan Police. Officers were acting on intelligence that the car was carrying a MAC-10 sub-machine gun, a fearsome weapon that can fire up to 1200 rounds a minute.

As the car was stopped, PC Tony Long, a very experienced firearms officer, stated that he saw Rodney duck down in the vehicle as if picking something from the floor, and, fearing this was a firearm, fired eight shots, six hitting Rodney, killing him. A later search of the car recovered three firearms, but no MAC-10 sub machine gun. The then Independent Police Complaints Commission investigated the case passing its findings to the Crown Prosecution Service who concluded, in July 2006, that there was insufficient evidence to charge any individual in respect of Rodney's death. Fifteen months of uncertainty for Tony Long and his family.

For various technical reasons it was ruled that an inquest enquiry into Rodney's death could not be held. But in May 2009, Rodney's Mother filed a case at the European Court of Human Rights, stating that her human rights had been breached because her son's death had not been properly investigated. This was despite the exhaustive investigations of the IPCC and the CPS. Four years of heart ache for the Long family.

In March 2010 a public enquiry into the shooting, under the Inquiries Act 2005, was announced. On the 3rd September 2012 the enquiry heard its first oral evidence. Almost seven and a half years of torment for Tony Long and his family.

In July 2013, the enquiry, chaired by Sir Christopher Holland, a former High Court judge, ruled that Tony Long had, "No lawful justification," in killing Azelle Rodney. The conclusion was that the first two shots had "neutralised" Rodney, the next six were unlawful. This is an amazing conclusion, that took Sir Christopher and his learned friends over three years of deliberation to decide. The actual incident, from the stop to the firing of the eighth shot by Tony Long, took a handful of seconds. Eight years of anxiety for the family of Tony Long, so far.

In July 2014 the CPS decided to charge Tony Long with the murder of Azelle Rodney. In July 2015 he was found not guilty by a jury. Tony Long, and his family, had endured over ten years of worry and anxiety, over an incident that played out in less than 3 seconds.

Everyone who's been a police officer knows why officers want to be firearms officers. They have more status, they don't deal with prisoners, they get better equipment, better uniforms. They drive BMWs and Mercedes, not Fords or Peugeots. They sample the adrenalin rush of confronting potentially armed criminals. But how long before these attractions are outweighed by the risks of a political decision to prosecute, even though the action was in good faith, leaving an officer vulnerable to the lottery of a friendly or hostile jury, prison, with all the physical risks that entails, loss of career and financial impoverishment for their family?

Already forces are finding it difficult to recruit firearms officer. The Telegraph reported in February 2024 that only six officers had applied in response to a recruitment drive by the Metropolitan Police, MO19, Specialist Forearms Command. If the "change," forecast by Michael J. Waldren, is an increase in the number of officers authorised to carry firearms, where will those officers come from, when they receive so little support when they're called upon to fire their weapons to protect the public?

Hands Up, Don't Shoot!

During the surreal Covid summer of 2020, the streets of Britain's cities were the scene of raucous demonstrations. Statues were toppled, obeisance on bended knee was demanded of all in authority. Politicians knelt, the clergy knelt, to their abiding shame some police officers knelt. British police officers, who don't carry firearms, were confronted by crowds shouting, "Hands up, don't shoot." "Black lives matter" came to be the mantra that no one could gainsay. What was the catalyst for this bizarre phenomenon? The death of a career criminal, George Floyd, during his arrest for passing a counterfeit bank note, in a city in the United States, four thousand miles away from London.

"When America sneezes, the whole world catches a cold." This phrase, apparently first used by Prince Metternich, the masterly nineteenth century Austrian diplomat, has certainly been true since 1945, when the USA stood as the only economic and military superpower, in the ruins of the post war world. But it's not the economic and military might of the United States that has had most effect on the rest of the world's culture, particularly on that of the Western world.

Hollywood, US television, pop music, have all had a profound influence on popular culture all over the world. US Cop shows from "Dragnet" in the fifties, through Hawaii Five-O in the sixties, Hill Street Blues in the eighties, right up to the excellent "Southland" and "The Wire" in the early years of this century, have been prominent on our screens for decades. There's plenty of gun play in all these shows. Such is the dominance of these series, that an uninformed person may think that British policing bears some resemblance to the action depicted. Hence the conflation of the two during the BLM summer of 2020.

On the face of it this is nonsense. US police kill around a thousand people every year. That figure has been very consistent for a number of years. British police may have to take the life of one person in a year, in most years, none at all.

In the year 2000 I went to the United States to study aspects of US policing on a scholarship scheme. I visited various departments from the NYPD to the LAPD, and I've been fascinated with American policing ever since. I wrote articles on US policing for a time for a UK police magazine. The United States is a unique country, and its policing is also unique. US police certainly have a reputation for being ready and willing to discharge their firearms, much too readily, some people will think. But, let me lay out some of the facts around police involved shootings in America, the picture is not as simple as it may appear.

On the evening of the 21st March 2024 Dexter Reed, a 26 year old black man was driving his SUV in the Humboldt Park area, on the West side of Chicago. He was pulled over by four officers from the local tactical unit, in plain clothes, but wearing vests declaring them to be police officers. The allegation is that Reed was not wearing a seat belt. Reed, who had previously been arrested, in July 2023, and charged with felony aggravated unlawful use of a weapon, refused to roll down the windows of his car when asked to do so by officers. It appears that he then discharged a firearm multiple times, wounding an officer in the forearm. The officers all retuned fire and, this is the part that will have UK firearms officers shaking their heads in disbelief, fired 96 shots, 13 of which struck Reed, killing him.

Reed's family has launched a Federal Civil Rights lawsuit against the city of Chicago. There have been demonstrations in support of the family, calling for the firing and prosecution of the officers involved. Even the Mayor of Chicago, the boss of the officers involved, opined at a press conference. "As Mayor and as a Father raising a family, including two black boys on the West side of Chicago, I'm personally devastated to see yet another young black man lose his life during an interaction with the police. My heart breaks for the family of Dexter Reed." With friends like these, who needs enemies?

During the weekend of the 13th and 14th of April 2024 an eight year old girl was shot and killed in Chicago, a one year old boy and an eight year old boy were among the eleven people wounded in the same incident. During the Easter weekend of 2024, 33 people were shot and 7 killed in Chicago. During the fourth of July weekend in 2021, 92 people were shot and 18 killed. This shocking death toll rolls on, week after week in the

Windy City. For these deaths there are no press conferences, no calls for Federal charges against the perpetrators or the city authorities. Almost none of these shootings will be carried out by the police. Many of these victims will be pedestrians, caught in the crossfire, or children asleep in their beds, the victims of stray bullets.

In 2023 there were 617 homicides in Chicago and 2,450 shootings, just under 2 deaths a day and nearly 7 shootings. England and Wales had 602 murders in 2022-23 in a population of 60 million. Chicago has a population of 2.7 million.

Chicago stands out because of its large total of murders and shootings, but the city has a large population, this forces the city down in the league table of murders per capita, that is murders per 100,000 of population. Murders per capita are higher in nine US cities than Chicago. St Louis, Missouri, with a population of 296,000, around that of Kingston Upon Hull, has the dubious honour of leading the pack on murders per capita, at 69.4 per 100,000 population. Chicago's rate is 18.26 and New York City's is 3.4. New Orleans, Baton Rouge, Dayton Ohio, Detroit, Baltimore and Birmingham, Alabama all have murder rates above 30 per 100,000. In 2022 the country with the highest murder rate in the world was Jamaica, at 53.34. So it appears that it's actually more dangerous to live in the most dangerous parts of St Louis, Missouri than in Jamaica. For context, England and Wales had a murder rate in 2020 of 1.0.

So, we've established that some areas of American cities are as dangerous as the most violent places in the world. Policing those areas will of course be a difficult and dangerous job. Policing in all of the United States carries special dangers as there is one firearm for every member of the 340 million population. Even domestic disputes are routinely settled with the threat, or use, of firearms, on account of their ready availability.

But what of the charge that US police target black people for special attention, and are more ready to use deadly force on African- Americans? Finding statistics on police use of force in the United States has been historically difficult for researchers. The FBI collect crime statistics, but traditionally these have not drilled down into police killings in a helpful manner. Since 2015, in response to the death of black youth, Michael Brown in

Ferguson, Missouri, the Washington Post began to compile a database of police shootings. This resource has become the primary repository of statistics on this subject. So, what does this database reveal?

In 2022 the police killed 1,095 people, as I've said a figure that is roughly consistent year on year. 254 of those killings were of blacks. Blacks make up 13% of the US population. If these police killings were consonant with population statistics this figure would only be 143. So, police are killing black people, almost exclusively black men, at 1.8 times the rate that would be expected. In contrast police killed 458 white people in 2022, or 43% of the total. Whites make up 71% of the US population, so whites are underrepresented in these statistics.

If the narrative, racist cops gratuitously killing black people, is accurate, then the question of whether black police shooting victims were armed is relevant. In 2023, 16 unarmed blacks were shot by the US police and the same number of whites, again a disproportion. Some of the unarmed deceased were killed in the act of reaching for a weapon, or other action threatening the lives of officers involved.

On the 23rd November 2023 Demarcus Brodie a forty-nine year old black man was shot and killed by an officer of the Fayetteville Police Department, North Carolina. Brodie had been subject of a traffic stop, and had engaged in fighting with the male and female officers. He was shot by the male officer as he began to overwhelm him. This is a prominent fear for US officers, to be beaten in a stand-up fight, and as a result to lose control of their weapon.

In July 2018, in Weymouth, Massachusetts, Officer Michael Chesna, was shot 10 times with his own weapon and killed. The offender had disabled him by hitting him with a rock. On the 21st July 2018 Fort Myers, Florida, Officer Adam Jobber-Miller was shot and killed with his own weapon, after a suspect involved in a cellphone theft knocked him to the ground, before grabbing his firearm. On the 29th December 2021, in Bradley, Illinois, Police Department Sergeant Marlene Rittmanic was executed with her own pistol, after first being shot and wounded, along with her partner, by black man, Darius Sullivan. The call had been to investigate a report of a dog barking in a car at a motel, and the shooting seemed motiveless. Sullivan took Sergeant Rittmanic's weapon as she lay wounded, after his own 9mm jammed, shooting her twice in the neck.

So why do the said black men die at a disproportionate rate to their share of the population? Is it out and out racism? Or is there another explanation?

According to FBI crime statistics in 2022 there were 19,776 homicides in the United States. 9,627, 49%, of them were committed by black offenders. If black people committed homicides in proportion to their population this figure would only be 2,570. On the other side of the equation, blacks make up 10,470, or 53%, of the homicide victims. Again this figure would be 2,496 if black victimisation was in proportion to their representation in the US population.

The picture painted by these statistics is clear. A very large number of American murders are carried out by young black men, in certain areas of American cities, the victims being other young black men. The causes for this put forward by commentators are many and various. The left may point to economic deprivation, lack of opportunity and systemic racism. The right to fatherlessness, gang wars, and a culture of violence in black communities. I'm not a social scientist, so I won't attempt to adjudicate on this discussion.

Will Sutton was a notorious bank robber in depression era America. When asked why he robbed banks he replied, "That's where the money is." I would venture that police disproportionately operate in areas where black youths commit homicide and carry illegal firearms, because that's where the crime is. I'm willing to bet that officers from the Chicago PD tactical unit pulled over Dexter Reed on that March night, not because of a seat belt offence, but because he was flagged as a person that had previously been charged with a firearms offence. If the police are proactively working to interdict armed criminals before they commit homicides, to get illegal guns off the streets, then they will inevitably come into contact with young men who are armed and dangerous. As the crime statistics don't lie this will mean that the police will disproportionately interact with young black men, in the areas of cities, where high numbers of murders take place.

As I write this I learn that four officers have been shot and killed in Charlotte, North Carolina, yesterday, the 29th April 2024. They were attempting to execute an arrest warrant for illegal possession of a firearm. Four other officers were also shot, but survived. The offender was eventually shot and killed by police. It is easy to criticise American police as "too gung ho," or "trigger happy" from this side of the pond. But people that engage in this criticism should try to walk a mile in the shoes of those they criticise. Perhaps in the shoes of Officer Jonathan Diller, shot and killed during a traffic stop in New York, on the 25th March 2024, or Officer Joseph McKinney, shot and killed while investigating a suspicious vehicle in Memphis, on the 12th April, or State Trooper Justin Hare, who was shot and killed on the 15th March when trying to help the driver of a broken down vehicle, West of Tucumcari, New Mexico, or Deputy Sheriff Greg McCowan, who was shot and killed during a traffic stop on the 8th February in Maryville, Tennessee. All killed doing their duty, all wanted to go home to their families. They, and all US police officers, deserve respect for risking their lives to keep the public safe.

Rot (Fiction. Or is it?)

Hilda and Bernard moved into their new council flat in the summer of 1954. It was the first time either of them had lived in a home with a bathroom, or an inside toilet. Bernard had just come back from national service in Korea. He had been a prisoner of the Chinese for two and half years. Hilda retrieved a very different man from the railway station, one wet Friday afternoon, from the one she had become engaged to, before she waved him off, from an equally rain drenched station, as he left for Korea in December 1950. But she was patient, and by the time they married, he had resumed working at the engineering works to which he was apprenticed before his national service. Although he still had episodes of withdrawal and moodiness, he was a good husband, as they settled into a domestic routine that they both found tolerable.

The estate grew through the fifties and sixties and, although they rarely had anything to spare, they got by and found pleasure in the friends that they made amongst the people that lived out their lives around them, who, for the most part, were working men along with their wives and children. These children, although boisterous and full of life, were always respectful and addressed Hilda as, Mrs Stout, as they passed her on the landings or the stairs. Although they both would have liked to have a family, Hilda and Bernard were not blessed with children, but their disappointment didn't diminish the satisfaction they felt in the gentle paths of their lives. They relied on no one, being good neighbours to any of their friends that might find themselves in temporary financial trouble, or in strife due to family disputes. They had no family nearby, their parents having died young, Hilda was an only child and Bernard's single brother had emigrated to Australia in 1957, on a ten pound ticket, along with a great many others.

Hilda and Bernard found happy companionship at the local social club. Bernard had been honoured to be elected to the committee in 1963. There were regular socials and dances, where the young people met and began romances, that often led to marriages and children that sustained the community. In the summers there were coach trips to the seaside, and to London to see the sights. Hilda and Bernard looked forward to these distractions from the beige background of their unexciting, but pleasantly satisfied lives. The 1960s are now seen as a time of rapid social change, but these great events, in the wider world, seem to barely touch the estate, or the people that lived there.

The area was patrolled by PC Roper. The big-framed, ex-navy man, had little need to even swing his ample bulk off the seat of his clunky black cycle, as his mere presence would invariably calm the rowdy youth, or quieten the inebriated husband, on his way home from The Red Lion, whose celebration at his triumph in the darts league, had become a little too boisterous.

The sixties rolled into the seventies. Hilda began to notice that the communal areas in the flats were not kept as clean as they had previously been. She swept and mopped her landing with the same enthusiasm, but most did not, and the council cleaners seemed to visit less frequently. On occasions bags of rubbish or discarded old carpets blocked the stairs. The grass areas between the blocks, where families used to meet and have picnics, were not maintained, becoming unsightly patches of mud in the winter, grainy deserts, when the sun shone in the hotter months. Flats were let to families within which there didn't seem to be a man, or those where a man did appear for a while, quickly to disappear, only to be replaced briefly by another. The children of these families were not as respectful to Hilda as she had previously expected. Sometimes they laughed at her when she asked them to move, so that she could pass them, as they loitered aimlessly on the stairs, smoking and making rude noises.

As the years of the eighties spun by, amidst talk of good times and greed being good, the estate took on a permanent veneer of shabbiness. No one took any notice of the no smoking signs screwed to the cracked plaster walls in the halls. Men hung around in the doorways selling, what Hilda was told, were drugs to emaciated wraiths that came from off the estate to buy, then lie in the halls to inhale smoke produced from lit baking foil, or openly insert needles into their skinny arms. Hilda and Bernard took to going out early to the local small supermarket, not venturing out at all after the hours of darkness. The social club membership dwindled, and the council withdrew their support, citing budget cuts. The building was boarded up, soon becoming covered in obscene graffiti. One night a group of youths set fire to it. There were said to be plans to rebuild it, but it lay for years, in sad dereliction, the notice board still standing with a dogged defiance, advertising long defunct chess clubs meets, forgotten Yoga classes.

Many, more prosperous, families had fled to the new estates on the edge of town as home-owners. The estate's decline continued without them. PC Roper retired, and was not replaced. If truth be told he'd been struggling to keep order for a while, as respect for the law nosedived, and much of his former authority, which was notional rather than actual, dependent on cultural acceptance of civilised norms, evaporated into disrespect and virtual anarchy. When police appeared on the estate they would arrive in cars, two at a time, and would soon retreat like a raiding party. The law and civilised order, held precariously in their hands, retreated with them.

Bernard had been laid off from his job in 1982, as the country tightened its belt, and he had found it difficult to find other employment. His health had been deteriorating for some time, a legacy of starvation and torture during his confinement in Korea. In June 1993 he passed away. Hilda, although she'd lost the love of her life, was able to carry on, as there were just enough of her old friends left to make life tolerable. But by the first decade of the twenty-first century all her friends were dead, or had been so incapacitated by the ravages of old age, that they had been confined to distant nursing homes, where their lives voices ebbed away into silence. By 2015, Hilda, now eighty-one years old, still in sound mind and body, was totally isolated in her flat, that was a still spotless island, in a sorry sea of rubbish, discarded needles and disrespect.

It had started with jeers and catcalls on the stairs as she ventured out to fetch her shopping and collect her pension. Groups of boys and girls, who seemed to eternally inhabit the stairs, landings and the hallways, at all times of day, even on school days, blocked her way, jostled her, and called her the vilest names. One girl had even spat on her from a higher landing. It was strange, she felt disappointed rather than frightened. She wished it would stop, but she didn't know what to do. In desperation she went to her GP to ask him. He advised that she call the police and the council. Hilda could only see trouble being caused by such a course. Hilda didn't want to cause trouble.

Prominent amongst the children, that haunted the halls and stairways, were a family of two boys and two girls, who lived with their mother in a flat two doors down along the same landing from Hilda. The Mother was a large pasty-faced woman, who was almost never seen, but when she was glimpsed through the window, as Hilda walked by, or when she was pacing up and down the landing, looking out as if expecting someone, dragging on a battered cigarette, she never spoke, or even acknowledged Hilda's existence. A sweet smell, like burnt leaves, had drifted around the landings for some years. But, after this woman and her kids moved in, the aroma had become ever present and unbearable. Hilda had tried to keep it out of her flat, but at times she sat in her living room feeling nauseous, powerless to resist the smell.

In the nineties the council had installed a door on the ground floor entrance to the flats. If the truth be known such a door had been required years before, with the numbers of all sorts of undesirables and rough sleepers, who had been using the public area for their own purposes. The door had worked quite well at first, as each resident was given a key. But when the keys were replaced by electronic fobs, it became clear that the door could be opened by administering a vicious kick. The boom of the door, being forced open at all times of night and day, became a feature of life in the flats. Hilda found herself lying sleepless in bed in the early hours, waiting for the booming of the door as it smashed against the wall. These, mainly nocturnal visitors, were customers of the drug dealers who occupied flats in the block, or were the homeless, looking for a dry place to spend the night.

These people often climbed the stairs to Hilda's floor. It appeared that the most prolific drug dealer in the block was the woman two doors down. Well, not her exactly, but a man that had moved in. A big man, with the look of violence about him, who seemed to spend all his time on the landing, glaring at Hilda with dark eyes, when she summoned the courage to venture out.

One day in despair she telephoned the council to complain about her situation. At first, she was told to use the pro forma on the council website to make her complaint. When she explained that she did not have a computer, she was told, by a young man that seemed in a hurry to get on and talk to someone else, to go to local library where staff would help her.

She had concluded, with a sort of strained hopelessness, that no one cared about her situation, when she received a phone call from a police officer, with a soft voice, who explained that she had been monitoring anti-social behaviour, that's what she called it, in Hilda's block. She had discovered that Hilda had called the police a few weeks before, about an altercation that had occurred between the big man and, what sounded to Hilda, like several other men on the landing outside her flat. The disturbance had been brief, but there were shouts and, what Hilda had concluded were cries of pain. On venturing out the next morning Hilda had discovered what looked like blood on the floor, and more blood smeared on the handrail of the stairs. She had called the police non-emergency number, and, after a very long wait, she had related what had happened to a nice young man who had given her an incident number. She had heard no more until now. The police officer asked permission to call on Hilda, with an official from the council, who also dealt with anti-social behaviour.

So the following Tuesday, as arranged, two women rang Hilda's bell, coming into her living room, where she offered then tea and rich tea biscuits. They both wore ordinary coats, so at first Hilda couldn't tell who was the police officer. But, over tea they introduced themselves, and Hilda could see that the younger of the two had a police top under her coat and, what she thought must be a radio, that looked like a mobile phone, in a holder on her chest.

"We know that you've been having trouble here with noise and other problems," said the older of the two, a woman with dyed blonde hair, gone almost yellow, with the roots growing out to grey, who had introduced herself as one of the council's anti-social behaviour team. "We want to help, but we need more evidence first."

Hilda was confused. She turned to the police officer. "Can't you just arrest the people that are causing the trouble here?"

The younger woman smiled. She had a flawless complexion and beautiful brown eyes. Hilda found herself liking her. Like a daughter that she had never had.

"I have no power of arrest. I'm a Police Community Support Officer."

"What is that?" Hilda asked.

"I gather intelligence from the community, and work in partnership to sort out problems," the beautiful girl replied. Hilda thought that she would have been a great match for a son that had never been born.

The council woman pulled out some papers from her briefcase, handing them to Hilda.

"These are diary sheets. Please fill in any incidents of ASB,"

"ASB?" Hilda asked.

"Anti-social behaviour. Noise, drug dealing, fighting, any violence that you may hear or see."

Hilda flicked through the sheets. They were divided into boxes for each day and there was a series of questions over each day. The type of behaviour heard and witnessed. Who were the offenders, how did the behaviour make the compiler of the diary sheets feel? When the tea was finished, the rich tea eaten, the pair disappeared back to the world from whence they came.

Hilda became an avid chronicler of the dystopian life in the public areas of the flats. Every noise in the night, every disrespect on the landing, every sad broken wraith lying blocking the hallway, was captured in a moment in time on her diary sheets.

Although her visitors had not been easily identifiable as authority figures, other residents must have gleaned who they were, as the morning after their visit Hilda had opened her front door to find excrement smeared across it. Dog or human, she couldn't tell, but, as she scrubbed away with a wet cloth and a bucket of water, someone shouted the word "grass" from the stairwell.

After three weeks she was concerned that she had not been contacted again by the council or police. She mailed her sheets to the address at the council that she'd been given, but still, after six weeks, there was no response. But she continued to fill in the sheets, in blue biro, as it seemed to bring some order to events that had no real order at all.

She telephoned the lady at the council, but was told that she was on leave, and would contact her when she returned. She heard no more. She called the police call centre, being told that the officer that had visited her had left the police. The lady, who had a nice voice, told her that she would make a log of the call and someone else would call her. No one did.

One evening, three months after the visit of the two ladies, Hilda sat in her easy chair, the one that her and Bernard had bought in a sale the summer that England won the World Cup, and thought about the life they'd shared together, and how it seemed, at the time, that this is how it would always be. An endless summer. The front door to the flats banged against the wall so hard that her window vibrated. There was shouting in the hallway, someone ran past her flat along the landing, there was the sound of smashing glass and drunken laughter. She turned on the television, there was a show about rich women in a sunny part of America. She turned up the volume as far as it would go.

What is to be Done?

In 1902, Vladimir Ilyich Ulyanov, known to history as Lenin, Father of the Russian revolution and Soviet Russia, published a work with the title, "What is to be Done?" This text promoted the forming of a vanguard of committed revolutionaries, to spread revolutionary ideas amongst the workers, thereby creating the conditions for revolution.

I decided to borrow this title for this final chapter of this book, as almost everyone concedes that the police service in this country is broken, or at least in need of fundamental reform. In this chapter I want to set out, what I believe has to be done, to set the conditions and measures to remedy this.

Fifteen years after the publication of his work Lenin, and his party, known as the Bolsheviks, came to power in Russia. They rode to power on the back of a disastrous war with Germany, and the collapse of the Tsarist autocracy. The October revolution of 1917 ushered in seventy-four years of repression and terror for the Russian people. The Bolsheviks had a clean slate upon which they could sketch their revolution. Lenin, Trotsky, then Stalin had no restrictions on what they could do to further the changes they desired in Russia society.

There is no blank slate upon which the revolution, or rather the retrogression that British policing requires, can be traced. It's clear that we must return to the principles first set out by Sir Robert Peel. I don't claim to be an oracle. I have thirty years experience, and a genuine interest in the history of policing, to call upon when I make these observations. I may be wrong, but I suspect most law-abiding people in the country, certainly almost all my contemporaries in the police, will agree with what I say.

Of course, John, many readers will declare. Society is very much different now that it was in 1829, when Richard Mayne set out the Peelian principles, or 1965, when Unit Beat Policing came to the fore, or even when you first trod the beat, in 1982. That's true, Britain has changed and is constantly changing. But the principle, that the majority of the public want a safe, tranquil society has never changed. People want to walk down the street at all times of night and day in safety. They want to feel that there are capable guardians to call upon when required. When this guardianship fails, and crimes are committed, they want victims to have the satisfaction of seeing the perpetrators of those crimes brought to justice, to receive an adequate and just punishment. Can anyone say, with a straight face, that this is the situation that we have at the present time?

Some are bound to say that my suggestions to change are harking back to an era that never existed. Britain in the nineteen fifties, sixties and seventies was racist, reactionary, devalued women, persecuted gay people. That's all true, but behind all that was a social tranquility that can be reimagined without the need to impose on it the baggage of all the rest of that stuff. What we have now, is a facade of universal tolerance, built on a societal quicksand of anti-social behaviour and lawlessness, blended with an unhealthy dose of cynicism.

The image of British policing is tarnished. Not a day goes by without some story of a corrupt officer, amongst the worst of whom are Wayne Couzens, the murderer of Sarah Everard, and serial rapist David Carrick. But it's also the seemingly small-scale failures, small in the round, but vitally important to the victim of that crime, or sufferer of that anti-social behaviour. The call back that never happens. The victim providing CCTV of an incident that's never acted upon. The long-suffering resident who gives up calling the police to report youths throwing stones at her car again, as they never respond, or respond with a disinterested shrug.

My prescription for mending the British Police service is simple. Genius plans often are. My script would read.

- Recruit the right people.

- Promote the right people.

- Put police back on the streets.

- Re-skill detectives.

- Get rid of useless box ticking and bureaucracy.

Recruitment

Twenty years ago, my wife and I took a trip to Prague, a wonderful medieval city, almost unique in central Europe, in that it was virtually untouched by the destruction of World War Two. We had arranged a transfer from the airport to our hotel. Our driver was a Canadian national, who'd lived in the Czech Republic for some years. It soon came out in conversation that I was a police officer, and in response our Canuck friend informed us that, in his opinion, Czech police were very corrupt, always taking money if offered. I immediately asked him if their pay was poor. "Of course," he admitted, "Very poor."

One of the spurs that made me want to join the police in 1982 was the attractive pay and benefits package offered at that time. Under the Edmund Davies pay reforms, as a new probationer, I was paid over £7,000 a year, a very good salary at the time. With increments this salary would increase with my policing experience. Along with this salary came the provision of a police house, free of rent or council rates, with an allowance to carpet and decorate the house. Free prescriptions, free dental care, free spectacles. If an officer was given permission to buy their own house, there would be a rent allowance paid, based on the rateable value of the purchased property. This rent allowance was uprated every two years, and was tax free, the tax paid refunded every May pay cheque. A great savings scheme!

If an officer was required to work at a station other than their own, an allowance was paid for subsistence. If overtime, amounting to more than two hours was worked, a refreshment allowance could be claimed. If the officer was sent away for a residential course, a nightly course allowance was paid.

These benefits came with some pretty stiff restrictions on the officer's personal life. The Chief Constable dictated where an officer could live. If they were posted to another town thirty miles away, the Chief would require them to uproot their family and move house. No arguments. Permission had to be sought to marry, the prospective wife's background undergoing intense scrutiny. No member of the officer's immediate family was allowed to be involved in any aspect of the licensing trade. Officers were not allowed to take up any other paid employment without the permission of the Chief Constable. I requested permission to write articles for the magazine "Police Review" in the mid-nineties, receiving a certificate from the Chief Constable, graciously giving me permission to do so.

Most of these benefits, that I enjoyed during my service are gone. Police houses, rent allowance, meal allowances, dentists fees, prescriptions payments, all gone.

My starting salary of well over £7,000 a year, in 1982, was a thousand pounds above the average annual salary paid that year. Added to that were the many fringe benefits that I have described above. In 2024 the starting salary for the police in the provinces is around £30,000 a year, £5,000 less than the average British salary and there are no additional benefits to cushion this blow. This salary does rise steeply after a few years, but many new recruits are not making it past even those first few years.

Many commentators suggest that the recruitment to the police of ex-service men and women is the answer to the problem of quality of recruit. The insistence, until recently, that new officers should have a degree, or study for a degree in their probation, has undoubtedly been off putting to many ex-service types. The self-discipline necessary in service life is certainly useful in the field of policing. I've known many ex-navy, army or air force in my time in the police. Many of them have made good practical bobbies, content to see out their service as PCs, or at most sergeants, remaining at the cutting edge of police work. There is no doubt that the ex-service supply chain was useful to the service.

During my last Police Federation conference in 2012, the policing minister in the Cameron government, Nick Herbert, blithely responded to a question from the floor on recruitment, stating that poor police starting pay wasn't an issue, as people were still applying to join in adequate numbers. Herbert is one of the many politicians that will defend generous pay rises for MPs because, "It's necessary to attract good people." Clearly this rule doesn't apply in the police service.

In 2010 Theresa May appointed Sir Tom Winsor, the ex-rail regulator, to enquire into police pay and working conditions. Winsor duly did the bidding of his mistress. He recommended savage cuts to police pay. The starting salary would decline by over £4,000 per annum, beginning at a measly £19,000. Winsor was soon rewarded for his work, being made the Chief Inspector of Constabulary in June 2012. He was seen parading around in police uniform, even though he had never spent one minute patrolling the streets, and has never made a single arrest. In 2015 he was knighted, proving that doing the bidding of the administrative state is more productive than exhibiting integrity.

Winsor and May's reforms soon paid dividends. Police numbers fell from a high of 144,000 in 2009 to just over 122,000 in 2018. This catastrophic loss of staff decimated neighbourhood policing teams, further reduced police patrol capability, a facet of policing that was already on life support. Calls went unanswered, community problems were neglected, public support, already in short supply, circled the bowl. In 2023 a survey carried out by the Policy Institute at King's College, London, found that 67% of respondents said that had a great deal or quite a lot of confidence in the police. This was down from 87% in 1981. In 2024 another survey, by the Economic and Social Research Council, found that only 40% of the people surveyed trusted the police. May has paid no price for her part in the undermining of England and Wales police. Made Prime Minister in 2017, she was ennobled in 2024, becoming Baroness May of Maidenhead. Failing upwards seems to be what politicians, and apparatchiks like Winsor, do.

Meanwhile police officers dealt with the poisoned chalice that Winsor and May had presented them with. A 2023 report, by the Social Market Foundation, found that police pay had declined in real terms since 2000.

"Analysis of ONS data on nominal pay for selected occupation and sector groups shows that police pay rose by 39% in total between 2000 and 2022, while inflation over the period was 67%, and average pay across all employees rose by 76%.

This equates to a total real-terms fall of 17% over the period, or 0.8 per cent per year."

Police pay had not only fallen against inflation, but officer's poor remuneration meant that they were an outlier in public sector workers, most of whom have done better.

A few months ago a video circulated on the internet showing a trainee officer, apparently working for the Greater Manchester Force, carrying out a stop search for drugs. The officer had a very thick, and what appeared to be African accent, and appeared to have some difficulty in speaking intelligible English. I'll add a caveat here. I can't verify that this video is genuine, as so much on the net nowadays is photoshopped or parody. But this did appear, to me anyway, to be kosher.

Here is a collection of anecdotes, but anecdotes that speak volumes about some of the people that have been recruited in recent years. Even Fifteen years ago, a friend of mine, a Chief Inspector, was in charge of the personnel matters in a policing division. He told me that two probationer constables had come to him in one day to resign. When asked why they had made this decision, both replied that they, "Didn't think the job would be so confrontational." I've seen multiple reports of new recruits resigning in the first few weeks of patrol training, as they didn't want to work night shifts or at weekends. Many thought that overtime was optional. A new constable asked for an additional rest day on his birthday. When refused, his parents stormed into the station to make a complaint to the shift inspector. I could go on. I won't even relate the tale of the officer that needed his "comforter" on board his panda car when he worked nights. Apocryphal? I'm assured not.

My point is simple. If you don't make a job attractive in terms of pay and benefits, the right people will go elsewhere, to jobs where they can enjoy a good salary and attractive benefits.

But it's not just attracting people to do the Job, it's also about retaining them. Policing, until recently, has always been a blue collar job. Young working-class men, ex-servicemen, attracted to the idea of a disciplined profession, with a public service ethos. Attempts have been made over the years to inject an academic element into the job, I applied unsuccessfully for the graduate entry scheme. The recently scrapped and ridiculous requirement for each recruit to have a degree, or to achieve one in the first few years of their service, is an indication that the Home Office still don't understand the basic nature of most police work. Policing at the street level is a skill that is acquired through experience, not by academic study.

In 2022 there were around 140,000 warranted police officers in England and Wales. Approximately 93% of these officers hold the ranks of constable or sergeant. I have heard countless stories of young people joining the police, expecting to rise rapidly up the ranks, only to be disappointed when this doesn't happen. Rather than accepting this fact, and trying to become efficient officers, they become disillusioned and resign. In 2023 the number of police officers resigning, prior to receipt of pension, overtook those retiring. Most of these officers were those that were very early in service.

The way to address this problem is to scale back efforts to exclusively attract academically minded recruits and revert, in part, to the recruitment to the young, practical minded person that might be considering a career in engineering, or plumbing, or nursing. This will only happen if the pay and conditions improve. Perhaps one day, in the near future, a large number of young men and women will answer an advertisement, not in the Guardian like me, but on some website, that explains that a police career holds out the prospect of a secure life for them and their family, and a satisfying career. I'm not hopeful.

Promotion

In his excellent record of the fall of the once greatest police force in the world, "Broken Yard. The Fall of the Metropolitan Police," investigative journalist, Tom Harper, tells of a DCI who received an agitated phone call from a Superintendent, with whom he was acquainted. It appeared that this Superintendent had to give evidence in court. His evidence was straightforward enough. That he'd ordered some PCs onto the roof of a premises to usher some person, who was at risk, down. Hardly controversial. The controversy was that this senior officer had never actually given evidence in court before. Unbelievably, he needed pointers on how to approach evidence giving.

A great many current senior police managers seem to have little experience of real police work as evidenced by the above anecdote. Few seem to have the stomach to venture out onto the streets to find out what their officers are really up to. A great many of them seem to have been promoted because of their immutable characteristics, or to satisfy some DEI quota. When they reach the top, they look for others who share their world view, thereby perpetuating such people at the top of policing.

In my chapter on senior officers I spoke of Maggie Blyth, who, after a career in the Probation Service, joined the Hampshire Constabulary as a direct entry superintendent in 2016. She moved to the post of Deputy CEO at the College of Policing in 2023 and has recently been appointed the interim Chief Constable of Gloucestershire Constabulary, after the former Chief Constable, Rod Hansen, had been suspended, following allegations of gross misconduct. I have never met Ms Blyth, and have no knowledge of her capabilities, or her personal qualities. But from entry to chief constable in eight years? I'm sure that Ms Blyth's credentials in respect of Diversity, Equity and Inclusion will be impeccable. Her bona fides in respect of LGBTQ rights will be beyond reproach.

The problem is that Ms Blyth has never walked a yard of beat in the pouring rain as a PC, never faced down the eighteen stone drunk on her lonesome, until help arrived. Never mothered a squad as their sergeant, never covered for one of the said squad, who had made an honest mistake, and now faced unfair consequences. Never supervised prisoners as a custody officer, never booked in ten prisoners from a fight at three in the morning. Never bossed a station as an inspector, never made a pressure decision at midnight when she's the only supervisor on their feet, in the whole force area. Never investigated any complex crimes as a DI or a DCI, never stood in the witness box all day, being cross examined by that wily KC. She has done none of these things. Not a perfect analogy, but it's like appointing someone as England football manager who has never seen a ball kicked in anger.

Of course, Ms Blyth will encourage the promotion of other senior officers in her image. Those skilled in the politics, masters and mistresses the art of mouthing the appropriate phrases, promoting the College of Policing approved initiatives. Dave Marshall in his book, "The Fall of Policing," sums up the problem. Senior officers today, "May be able to write an impressive DEI strategy or action plan, be able to talk endlessly about the injustices of underrepresentation in the service and what they plan to do in righting the social wrongs, and discuss the ills of all the misogyny and sexism that pervades policing. However, ask them to run an effective anti-crime operation and you'll see a load of rabbits in headlights just before you see a cloud of dust as they beat a hasty retreat."

So, how is this remedied? The College of Policing is the most influential body in setting the standards for policing. There appears to be no prospect of any change to the qualities seen as prerequisites for senior officers from that direction. Other chief constables? Of course not, they are all cut from the same cloth.

The HMIC, the Inspector of Constabulary? The execrable Tom Winsor, served as Chief Inspector of Constabulary between 2012 and 2022. His successor, Andy Cooke, is at least a police officer, the ex-chief constable of Merseyside, unlike Winsor, who should have been arrested for impersonating a police officer. I have no personal knowledge of Mr Cooke, or his attitude to the new sacred cows of policing, like diversity and inclusion. I strongly suspect that he wouldn't have climbed so high, unless he pledged at least some fealty to them.

So, who can save us, as the commanding heights of policing seems to have been lost to the new barbarians? I'm afraid it probably comes down to politics.

I think that the only hope is a Home Secretary that understands the problems, is willing to take on the policing blob, and start to get real police officers, skilled in the arts of patrol, crime prevention and detection back to the top of the ladder. But who will do this? The current Home Secretary, Yvette Cooper, not a chance? What about any of the Home Secretaries spanning my time in the Job, the patrician Willie Whitelaw, in 1982, to the useless and destructive Theresa May, in 2012? There were fourteen of them. Most of them were instantly forgettable, like Kenneth Baker in the early nineties, whose only claim to fame was the ridiculous and unworkable Dangerous Dogs Act 1991, or Jacqui Smith, who was forced to resign in 2009, due to inaccuracies in her expenses claims. Some were openly anti-police like Theresa May, or Kenneth Clarke who enthusiastically sponsored the Sheehy vendetta. None of them gave any indication that they understood the need for the police to return to first principles. I foresee dark times ahead.

Put Police back on the Streets

There's not a great deal to be written about this. Divert officers from whatever nebulous nonsense that they're doing, putting them back on patrol, preventing crime and disorder. Routine activity theory. Capable guardian on the streets = less crime and disorder.

Set a percentage of the force strength allocated to patrol and neighbourhood policing, In respect of my own force, 10% of the force allocated to patrol and neighbourhood policing would be 140 at any one time. Depending on the shift system this would require 560 officers allocated to patrol and neighbourhood policing including sergeants and inspectors. This would be under a four-shift system. One shift earlies, one shift lates, one shift nights and one shift rest day. The small stations could operate a three-shift system, that requires fewer officers, as nights and lates are split between one squad. Traffic, dog section and ARVs would be on top of this, perhaps another 200 officers. That would leave 640 officers to do the rest, CID, custody, senior officers etc.

Based on the parlous state that front line uniform policing was in when I retired in 2012, and knowing that patrol numbers have been since then, I would estimate that there's only a third of the 140 I deem essential for the safety of the public on the streets of Dorset at any one time in 2024. I am an evangelist for the return of proper preventative patrol to the streets of England. Unfortunately, I'm also a pessimist. Preventative patrol was abandoned for the reasons that I've already stated in this book. The culture change, that would herald its return, is not on the immediate horizon.

Re-skill Detectives

Throughout this book I've stressed that the primary job of the police is to prevent crime. But some crime will always happen, and when it does, it's necessary to thoroughly investigate it, charge an offender and place him before a court if at all possible. This is necessary both in the interest of justice, and so that law abiding citizens feel that there is sanction meted out on those that disrespect the law.

Tabloid newspapers are replete with stories of how police refuse to investigate many crimes, even when the complainant had CCTV of the offence. Even when they have investigated the crime themselves and located the stolen property, there are many stories of police still refusing to act. This is due to laziness and/or poor supervision. When crime screening, sifting out crimes, where there is little physical or witness evidence so that they will not be investigated, came in the late nineties, I was uneasy as I knew that some officers would take the path of least resistance, opting to write up the crime in such a way that it would be screened, thus saving them work. Again, this is due to poor supervision.

Such laziness seems to have become institutionalised. In September 2023 the Co-op's Campaign and Public affairs Director, Paul Gerrard, told the Daily Mirror that in 80% of cases where their security guards had detained a shoplifter, the police fail to attend. This is appalling in itself, but could be remedied by a change of attitude of senior management.

But there is a more serious problem facing forces. The lack of experienced detectives to investigate serious crime.

My experience in the police between 1982 and 2000 at least, was that the CID ran the force. Detectives had a better chance of being promoted, were looked upon favourably for the plum jobs, and were generally regarded as superior in every way to their uniformed colleagues. I remember a Detective Chief Superintendent addressing a meeting, while I was attached to CID in 1996, declaring that, "Elitism is good and the CID are the elite." In the early 2000s, as a uniform inspector I was considering applying for a job as an inspector on Special Branch, the unit that deals with subversion and terrorism. I knew the Superintendent in charge of SB, we'd worked together many times. I telephoned him and, although he conceded that he knew I could do the job well, he couldn't consider me, as I wasn't a detective inspector.

Operation Midland was a Metropolitan Police operation to investigate the allegations of sexual offences and murder made by a man named Carl Beech. In 2014 Beech made a number of allegations against prominent people such as former Home Secretary Leon Brittan, former Prime Minister Edward Heath and former Chief of the Defence Staff, Lord Bramall. Beech claimed that these men, and others, had run a VIP child abuse ring. In addition Beech claimed that a member of parliament, Harvey Proctor, had stabbed a twelve year old boy, before strangling him to death. In addition, at least two other children were killed for sexual pleasure.

The detective leading the investigation, Detective Superintendent Kenny McDonald, described Beech's allegations as "credible and true." But despite high profile raids on the homes of the suspects, at great damage to their personal standing, no evidence was found to corroborate any of Beech's allegations. Operation Midland was terminated in 2016 with no charges against any of the suspects named by Beech.

An enquiry into the investigation by Sir Richard Henriques, a retired judge, found that detectives were too willing to believe Beech's uncorroborated allegations, concluding that his story was consistent, when it was clearly not. Officers also obtained warrants to search the accused premises under false pretences. The conclusion reached was that the investigating detectives were not rigorous enough in their examination of Beech's allegations, and perhaps too naive in believing him at an early stage in the investigation.

Following an investigation by Northumbria Police, in May 2019, Beech was found guilty of twelve counts of perverting the course of justice and fraud. He was sentenced to eighteen years in prison. During the investigation it was revealed that Beech was also under investigation for possessing indecent images of children and voyeurism. Northumbria Police also discovered documents that proved that Beech was a fantasist, who played out scenarios of being a victim of child sexual abuse.

It is inconceivable that this investigation would have progressed as far as it did twenty years ago. Senior experienced detectives, many of whom would have progressed to very senior ranks in the force, would have exercised reasonable scepticism of Beech's allegations, long before the reputation of prominent politicians and military figures had been dragged through the dirt.

There is a national shortage of detectives. In surveys detectives spoke of high case levels and the punishing stress of constant pressure to bring cases to court. Uniform work can also be highly stressful, but the role of a DC, once sought after and prized, as a step up from a uniform constable, no longer has that pull. In 2019 a report by HM Inspectors found that 14% of all detective places in England and Wales were unfilled.

In a survey detective respondents cited high work-loads, inability to switch off, due to prolonged and complex investigations and burn out, as reasons why they were considering leaving the CID. Attempts to bolster the detective numbers with direct entry candidates has had mixed results. In her 2023 book "No Comment, What I Wished I'd Known About becoming a Detective," Jess McDonald describes how she joined the Metropolitan Police as a direct entry detective, after gaining a degree in Ancient History and French, then drifting without direction through various jobs. Her experience in the Met was not a good one. Her book, over page after page, exhibits why candidates who have never experienced the Job, from the uniform bottom up, rarely have the stomach for the long haul. Ms McDonald abandoned her new profession in short order, claiming that she was bullied by her supervisor, although my reading of her position was that supervisor was merely doing his job. Jess McDonald clearly exhibits her misunderstanding of the nature of the police as a disciplined service, when she mischaracterised a request for her to work overtime as optional, "Although theoretically you should be asked whether you want to stay or not." She blithely declares.

The Police Federation is lukewarm to this scheme. The Deputy Chair of West Midland Police Federation, Jason Dooley, himself an experienced Detective Sergeant, pointed out that in the past, "You had to be of a certain experience or a police officer who was proven on the streets, investigating stuff, talking to the public and talking to the criminals as well, and gaining information from people." He went on to say, "I fear we might be setting up people to fail."

But it's not only at the investigatory level that CID experience is vital. Trained investigators that understand the pressures and technicalities of investigating serious crime, are no longer rising to the most senior ranks in the police. Current senior officers are managers, not leaders, people that have learned how to say the right thing, exhibit the right attitude in the diversity, equity and inclusion swamp.

Roy Ramm, not only has an excellent surname, that implies his hard charging credentials, but he was also a seasoned detective that rose to the rank of Commander in the Met, in charge of Specialist Operations. In his book "Broken Yard," Tom Harper writes of Ramm's disquiet at the quality of current senior officers. Ramm commented, "They are professional police managers who have risen through the ranks without trace, without ever standing in the witness box and giving evidence. This breed of political senior officers has done immense damage to policing."

There is a need to re-skill detectives at the investigating level of DC to DI. As an almost exclusively uniform man it sticks in my throat to suggest that one of the incentives to encourage the right people to want to be detectives may be financial. It speaks volumes about how far the police service has advanced miles down the wrong path, that this is even necessary.

At the senior level, chief superintendent and above, it's vital that both experienced uniform officers and detectives make it to the most senior ranks. Concerns with the ethnic make-up of the force, or the sexual orientation of the work force, or the force's ability to influence the social attitudes of the public are unimportant, when set against the need to ensure public tranquility and safety.

Get Rid of Useless Box Ticking and Bureaucracy

It's 1984. I arrest a man who's drunk and has been shouting at passers by, and has told me to "Fuck off," when I warn him to quieten down. The offence is Drunk and Disorderly under the Criminal Justice act 1967. I place him in front of the station sergeant, this was pre-PACE, so there's not a custody officer. He's searched and put in a cell. I have to do some paperwork, as prior to PACE many minor offenders are kept in custody for court the next day.

I complete a white cardboard folder with his details. I write a summary of the offence, a summary that the prosecutor will read to the magistrates in court the next morning. I write a short statement of arrest. I check him on the Police National Computer, telephone the Criminal Records Office at Scotland Yard for his last three convictions, if he has any. I put all this in the folder, the work of an hour at most. I'm then back out on patrol keeping the public safe and preventing crime. At six am I go home to bed. My arrest is taken to the local court by early turn officers, where a prosecutor, usually a police inspector for minor offences, relates the story to the magistrates, The man will almost always plead guilty, being subjected to a small fine. End of story. The system works well for everyone.

Then came the advent of the Police and Criminal Evidence Act 1984. Then came the Prosecution of Offences Act 1985, the legislation that heralded the setting up of The Crown Prosecution Service.

Straight away a voluminous Manual of Guidance, with a bewildering number of associated forms, turned the process I described above into a bureaucratic quagmire. A simple Drunk and Disorderly, or a straightforward theft from a shop, was transformed, from a simple, easily traversed procedure, into a nightmare of form filling and box ticking. In my force Admin Support Units were set up in the early nineties. These were intended to take much of the mundane paperwork away from frontline officers, but they simply became a different set of people telling officers what forms to fill in. Theory tells us that bureaucracies work to perpetuate their power, setting in place complex rules and arcane procedures. This was certainly the case with ASUs and the CPS.

As a Sergeant in the nineties I took to calling the labyrinthine memorandums from force bureaucracy, "Communiques from the Planet Zog." I would read them to the open-mouthed officers on parade, and literally none of us would gain any useful knowledge from the experience. I remember one particular entry on force General Orders concerning the "severity scores" of various offences. It was absolute gobbledegook, being surely intended more to exhibit the faux expertise of the sender, than to convey any useful information to the troops on the ground.

Through the nineties, and into the new century it became the mantra that the police service should do all it could to reduce bureaucracy. But nobody did any work to even set the service on the road to this, let along achieve that goal.

It's true that police forces have traditionally played fast and loose with crime statistics. Back in the latter years of the twentieth century, if three burglaries occurred in an area in one night, the DI would classify them as one "continuing crime." Of course, if they were detected, they would miraculously turn back into three crimes. Crime stats' were manipulated to a certain extent, but it was a benign, bureaucratic exercise, that harmed no member of the public.

Then the government became obsessed with the proper counting of crimes, on the face of it a noble cause. Despite the Blair government placing more emphasis on the British Crime Survey, that measured the public's perception of crime, and self-reporting rather, than official statistics. Forces were told that Her Majesty's Inspectors would come down hard on forces that didn't conform rigidly with Home Office crime recording rules. So what did they do? They fell back on the only strategy that bureaucracies have in their arsenal. They created an additional bureaucracy to secure compliance. My own force appointed a force crime scrutineer, or auditor, I don't remember the exact nomenclature. That person was minutely trained in counting rules, being tasked to go through all incidents with a fine-toothed comb, to ensure that all crimes that could be recorded were recorded.

Consider this scenario. It's 1984. A fight occurs between two groups of young men, on a deserted street in the early hours. No participant is seriously injured. The police are called, an incident log is opened on the force computer incident log system. Yes, Dorset did have such a system in 1984. Officers arrive as the fight is coming to an end, punches are still be thrown, but this ceases immediately on police attendance. No party to the incident wants to talk to officers. Police tell both groups to fuck off in opposite directions (that would be the tone of the words in those days) and anyone that wanted to continue the altercation would be arrested. Both groups move away and peace reigns. Officers tell control room that no offences have been disclosed, causing the incident log is be closed. No crime is be recorded. End of story, for that night at least.

Move forward thirty years. Sons of the 1984 antagonists fight on the same street, over some obscure beef that's travelled down through the ages. They've punched each other, a witness has seen this. When police arrive neither side wishes to speak with officers. You may think that the officers would read them their fortune and send them on their way, just as their Fathers had been advised three decades before. But now there are force crime scrutineers or registrars, or whatever highfalutin title that's been adopted. They're armed with their Manual of Home Office Crime Counting Rules. Such a practical denouement to this incident is not for them. Under their fiat this would now have to be recorded as two crimes, an assault on each. Officers would have to obtain details, return to the station to input the crimes, justifying why now arrests were made. All time away from patrol. All time away from pursuing the first, and most important of Peel's Principles, the prevention of crime.

I'm assured by someone, who still has day to day contact with police, that today's officers would not even know how to resolve this situation in a practical manner. It wouldn't occur to them to do so. Why would they, they've never been taught by the wily career PC, as I was, nearly half a century ago.

How would we break away from this situation, where bureaucracy clearly trumps the requirements of public safety?

This would require a chief constable to declare that they eschew this procedure, prioritising police visibility over bureaucracy. They would risk criticism from His Majesty's Inspectorate, and perhaps, opprobrium from their Police and Crime Commissioner. This, very desirable situation, is probably not going to happen, bearing in mind the conformist mindset of most current senior officers. But this is a nettle that must be grasped in the end, or the only future is unsafe streets and endless disorder.

Epilogue

So, this is where I stand. Somewhere during my service, but probably during the 1990s, the police service in England and Wales made a wrong turn. It became received wisdom that patrolling, particularly on foot, was a waste of time, also that the police don't have the resources to do that anymore. These misassumptions grew from the impetus to impose Unit Beat Policing, at any cost, in the sixties, and a belief that there was always something sexier, more important that should be prioritised over wandering around, having cups of tea with shopkeepers, and chit-chatting to little old ladies, and speaking to street people about what was going on in the local area. The main thrust of my argument is that public tranquility rests on the police doing exactly all those, "wandering around," things.

My wife and I visited China in 2019. On our itinerary were the sprawling gateway to China, Shanghai, the capital Beijing, the old imperial capital, Xi'an and of course the pandas at Chengdu. Everywhere we went felt safe, there were police officers on almost every street corner. But wait, you may say, you're not suggesting that we, in Britain, adopt the tactics of such a repressive regime, in order to bring law and order back to our streets. No, I'm surely not.

The second city we visited was Suzhou, around seventy miles from Shanghai. It's a city of beautiful bridges, canals and gardens, but it has a population of thirteen million, hardly a rural backwater. We stayed in a beautiful hotel well within the city. Each night of the three we stayed there, my wife and I would walk out into the congested narrow streets of the old city. We were the only Westerners on show, but we never at any point felt under threat or in any danger.

In Shanghai there had been a multitude of very unfriendly looking police officers, on every corner, armed with a long prong like devices, that were obviously designed to pin a person against a wall by their neck. These police officers wore very militaristic uniforms, and stood glaring at passers-by with a, "Don't mess with me," look on their faces. But, as my wife and I walked the evening streets of Suzhou, there was a very different police presence. Officers in Castro type caps and light brown uniforms, leaned on street corners, sat on walls, taking tea with locals, smiling and nodding at us as we passed by. They were relaxed and more approachable. I was sure that these officers knew everything that was going on in their area. The locals seemed happy to speak with them, and I'm sure they asked them for their help when trouble called. There was a definite feeling of peace and tranquility in the air. This was no repressive occupying army, but a genuine cadre of "Citizens in uniform." It's ironic that, in this small corner of authoritarian China at least, the principle of "The police are the public and that the public are the police," had taken hold, when it has so disastrously been abandoned in the land where that concept was conceived, nearly two centuries ago.

We must return to that principle if we are not to further slide down into the pit of public alienation from the police who should be keeping them safe. Naysayers may affirm that, there's no going back, ARVs are vital, specialist squads are needed to address specialist problems, body armour, Tasers and incapacitant sprays are essential for officer safety. Yes, I agree. The country is a mess, and all those aids are necessary. But it's also possible to accept that, but also return to the old ways of patrol. Of my five suggestions for the rejuvenation of policing, this is the most important. Get those officers back onto the beat, on foot, to re-engage with people, to get to know their troubles, and work with them to solve their community problems, but most of all, to prevent crime. It's what the police was created to do.

I'll leave the last words to Robert Reiner, Emeritus Professor of Criminology at the Law School of the London School of Economics, and one of our most distinguished academic thinkers on matters of the police and public safety. In the preface to the third edition of his masterful work, "Politics and the Police," Professor Reiner acknowledges that police are needed, "To deal with conflicts, disorders and problems of coordination which are necessarily generated by any complex and materially advanced social order." But the police are not responsible for creating those maladies that infect the social order. The police did not create poorly educated children, broken families, an obsession with consumerism, or mass estrangement from civil society. Are we asking too much that police are required to be the sole means to mend these breakages? As Professor Reiner observes.

"Good policing may help preserve social order: it cannot produce it. Yet increasingly this is what is being demanded of the police."

www.ingramcontent.com/pod-product-compliance
Lightning Source LLC
Chambersburg PA
CBHW070759040426
42333CB00060B/1226